An English Fan Abroad

Euro 2000 and Beyond

Kevin Miles

This book is dedicated to Sandra,
who more than anyone ensured that it would be completed,
mainly by spending my advance.

First published in Great Britain in 2000 by Rebel Inc,
an imprint of Canongate Books Ltd,
14 High Street, Edinburgh EH1 1TE

10 9 8 7 6 5 4 3 2 1

Rebel Inc series editor: Kevin Williamson
www.rebelinc.net

British Library Cataloguing-in-Publication Data
A catalogue record for this book is available upon request
from the British Library.

ISBN 1 84195 066 1

Typeset by Palimpsest Book Production Limited,
Polmont, Stirlingshire
Printed and bound by Omnia Books Limited, Glasgow

Contents

EURO 2000
On The Road

An English Fan Abroad

KEVIN MILES spent the summer working for the Football Supporters' Association (FSA) as co-ordinator of their Fans' Embassy at Euro 2000. He led a team of two other staff members and over a dozen volunteers providing an advice and information service to England's travelling support in Belgium and Holland, and acted as a media spokesperson on behalf of the FSA.

The FSA is a membership-based national supporters' organisation, founded in 1985 after the Heysel disaster to give a voice to football fans. It is a democratic body, with a national committee (of which Kevin is currently a member) elected at its policy-making annual conference. The FSA campaigns on issues of relevance to football fans and liaises on their behalf with the football authorities, government departments, police forces and other agencies.

The FSA first organised an embassy service for travelling England fans at the World Cup in Italy in 1990, and has developed the concept at subsequent international tournaments. In Euro '96 in England, they established, with financial backing from the Football Trust, fans' embassies in each of the host cities for visiting foreign fans. For the World Cup in France 1998, the FSA secured major commercial sponsorship for the first time, and organised a highly successful mobile embassy service which accompanied England fans around France. Kevin Miles served as full-time co-ordinator for the France '98 embassy, and co-authored the organisation's report into fans' experience of the tournament.

The FSA built on the experiences of these previous tournaments to provide an enhanced service for Euro 2000. Working for the first time in conjunction with the National Federation of Football Supporters' Clubs and in collaboration with members of the England Members' Club, the FSA demonstrated the commitment to unity among football fans' groups which has underpinned the growth of the umbrella group, the Coalition of Football Supporters. Once again the FSA worked in partnership with a commercial sponsor (the mobile phone company One 2 One, with whom the organisation has an ongoing and developing relationship), to provide a mobile embassy service.

With additional support from the *Sunday Mirror*, the embassy also produced a free fanzine, and in partnership with the website Football365 was also able to offer a 'virtual embassy' facility.

Since the tournament, the FSA has been engaged in campaigning and lobbying on behalf of those fans innocently arrested and deported from Belgium, and has secured assurances from the Government and the FA alike that arrest and deportation from Euro 2000 alone will not be deemed grounds for banning from future travel. The FSA has also been invited to take part in a new government working group to address the issues of England's fans abroad.

Membership of the FSA is open to any football fan. Details are available by phoning 020 8541 3399, or by writing to: FSA, 3/5 Grove Crescent, Kingston upon Thames, Surrey, KT1 2DR.

Kevin Miles is a writer and broadcaster, but first of all a football fan. He presents *Early Doors*, the Saturday lunchtime football programme on BBC Radio Five Live that has become essential listening for match-going fans.

Kevin lives on Tyneside with his wife Sandra and their four children, and remains a season-ticket holder at St. James's Park.

Acknowledgements

THIS BOOK CONTAINS a version of events at Euro 2000, and opinions formed on the basis of those events, for which I alone can be held responsible; they do not necessarily reflect the policies or views of the Football Supporters' Association, or indeed of anybody else. In fact by the time you read this, they may not even reflect my own views.

While I will quite cheerfully accept responsibility and even blame for what is written here, the credit for this book appearing at all deserves to be much more widely spread. There are loads of people who have earned the right to be thanked for their help and support, and I am bound to forget many of them, so if you think you helped in any way and you are not mentioned here, thanks very much anyway.

I would however like to extend particular thanks to the following people, whose contribution and assistance has been so vital that even a dozy git like me can't fail to include them.

The FSA Euro 2000 Fans' Embassy volunteer team: Peg Alexander, Jim Blanden, Alan Bloore, Adam Brammer, Gavin Burnage, Barry Dewing, Jane Edwards, Glen Gibson, Rachael Loftus, Cathy Long, Fiona McGee, Brian McNally, Jon Parker, Heidi Pickup, Alison Pilling, Paul Ray, Paul Thomas and Peter Warren.

All of the above contributed to making the Embassy the successful venture it turned out to be. For their particular help in writing this book however, I'd especially like to thank: Alison Pilling, who not only encouraged and cajoled me, but also proof-read it and even wrote a chapter herself; Cathy Long, who was constantly interrupted in her work of taking up the issue of the innocent deportees with requests for information; Paul Thomas and Rachael Loftus. Among the many other FSA members to whom I'm grateful, I'd also like to thank Malcolm Clarke, Steve Powell, Phil Rowley and Ben Tegg. Thanks also to all those England fans whose Euro 2000 experience was ruined by the Belgian police, and who have allowed their testimony to be reproduced here.

Other people I'd like to embarrass by singling them out would include BBC Radio Five Live's Gordon Farquhar and Paul Greer. Jon Zilkha showed me how to start, and Mark Sandell must take a large part of the blame/credit, as writing a book was his idea in the first place, albeit two years earlier.

Lots of others helped me get through the process of completing the book, and you know who you are. Just so everybody else finds out too, let me mention David and Katharine Miles, Liam and Rachael Thompson, Kevin Williamson, Mandy Chester, and Jackie Hughes. It's only fair too that great credit is given to Anita Anand.

I'd also in conclusion like to mention Andy Costello, Ged Grebby and Phil Jeffries. Not that they helped particularly, they're just my mates, and I know they'd like to see their names in print.

Kevin Miles
September 2000

Going Home?

JUNE 21st FELT like it would live up to its billing as the longest day, and it was still only 8.00am. That morning-after feeling, but this time the hangover was not brought on by alcohol. England were going home.

Sometimes when I have woken up with a real hangover, I've been able to look back on the night before and pinpoint the moment – or even the pint – when it all started to go wrong. Not that the hours – or pints – before and even after didn't contribute just as much to the discomfort as the one singled out for attention and blame.

This morning, it wasn't hard to identify a football equivalent of the dodgy pint. Philip Neville, and his unnecessary, ill-conceived and crudely executed attempt at a tackle late in the game. The one that conceded the penalty from which England could not recover. The one that cost us the single point needed to progress to the knockout stage. Romania were through. And Philip Neville had given me a hangover.

At its height, the party had been great. The previous Saturday night had been as good an atmosphere as I have ever experienced at a football match in some thirty years.

A bold statement, but I have thought long and hard about it, and I can't think of a better one. It's not as though there weren't candidates, all drawn from following Newcastle United through a long and less than glorious era.

The end-of-season promotion celebration on May 9th 1993, the party at St. James's to celebrate Premiership status with a light-hearted 7–1 victory over Leicester.

The end of the FA Cup 3rd round replay at Ewood Park two seasons later, the evening of Hottiger's banana and Lee Clark's winner, when we stayed behind for a good three-quarters-of-an-hour to sing 'Walking in a Keegan Wonderland'.

And of course, the too-good-to-be-true feeling after the famous 5–0 massacre of Manchester United in October 1996, the perfect revenge for ... well, never mind what for, just the perfect revenge.

Great experiences, all of them, but Saturday night had been special. And Newcastle weren't even playing. It was England. England against Germany. An England victory over Germany. The first England victory over Germany in a major competition for 34 years. This was a rare and special occasion, and the mood reflected it.

It was as if, in the unlikely setting of a provincial Belgian town, all those years of accumulated disappointment had at last found a release. This was not just singing and chanting I was hearing, but an outpouring of joyful emotion. Below me, shadows danced on the pitch in time to *The Great Escape* signature tune; not just my imagination coming over all poetic, but a consequence of the way the lighting gantry above us was shaking. The whole stand was swaying as thousands of England fans in the 'official' England end – as distinct from the two unofficial but no less 'England' sides – bounced and danced in celebration.

The mood was buoyant, ecstatic even, without malice. Thousands of football fans, from all areas of England, the full spectrum of club allegiances, united behind one cause. Deeply ingrained rivalries not forgotten but set aside, reflected in the St. George's flags displayed now around the ground, as they had been earlier around the Place Charles II. The names of different clubs, towns, even pubs all displayed – some stitched, some painted, but all on the same unifying background. It was impossible not to be affected by it. Any residual Geordie doubts I may have had about getting caught up in this particular patriotic fervour around Team England had long since – well, a good forty minutes since – been expunged by the fact that it was one of ours, our very own Alan Shearer who'd headed the crucial, historic goal.

And as with all the very best celebratory occasions, there was a song to go with it, one that I'll always associate with that game. Some ten minutes before the end of the match, just at the point where the euphoria at the scoreline was mixing with the nervous fear that there was still time for it all to go horribly wrong, to produce an intoxicating, exhilarating, almost overpowering tension, there was a tannoy announcement. It was something, intended helpfully, to the effect that an extra train had been arranged for after the match, heading for Ostend. Almost immediately it was met with a spontaneous reply, from a choir of thousands, of a chorus to the tune of 'Knees Up Mother Brown'. A fitting riposte, on more than one level: 'We're not going home, we're not going home, we're not going, we're not going, we're not going home!'

And now, four days later, on the contrary, they *had* all gone home. The Place Charles II was depressingly back to normal. The one or two bar owners setting out their plastic tables and chairs, ready for a new day's trade, served only to draw attention to how deserted the square was. The sun was shining and the fountains were in full flow, but to me, they may as well have been tumbleweed drifting across in front of me. It was business as usual. The dreams were over, England *were* going home.

With an hour to kill, I sat myself at a table in one of the

cafés overlooking the main square. As if to prove that my spirit of optimism had not been completely extinguished, I ordered a cup of tea, still prepared to believe that I may have stumbled across the only place in Belgium whose concept of tea was remotely similar to mine. As the waiter arrived with a cup of formerly hot water and a box containing maybe a dozen different sorts of 'tea bags', I knew I'd been kidding myself. I passed over the fruit flavours on offer, and opted for one calling itself 'English Breakfast Mixture'. At least its intentions were good, even if its taste proved not to be.

That morning, the *Daily Express* proclaimed 'We're coming home. But as England go out, the rest of Europe says good riddance.'

As I sipped my tea — without the accompanying cream — I picked up a newspaper from the table next to me. A local paper, *La Nouvelle Gazette* I believe it was called. *Riot? What Riot?* was the headline. 'The war of Charleroi never happened' was the opening sentence.

They couldn't both be right. This is how I saw it.

How Others See Us

I WOULDN'T PRETEND for a minute that my experience of Euro 2000 was typical of the travelling England fan. I did a fair amount of travelling before the tournament got under way, yet none of it involved going to see any of the qualifiers – with one exception. I was lucky enough, if that's the word, to be present at the second leg of the play-off against Scotland. No, not the efficient 2–0 victory at Hampden, but the Wembley game, that dismal affair that we lost 1–0. Best forgotten, but there are still one or two things that stick in the mind.

I remember trying, in vain, to salvage some consolation from the fact that the scorer of the only goal of the game was a Geordie, Don Hutchinson from Gateshead, Newcastle fan. It didn't help.

For all my best efforts, I can't forget how woeful England were down the left-hand side of the pitch. Crying out for a naturally left-sided player. Not words I thought I'd ever find myself uttering, but come back Graeme Le Saux. Or even John Beresford, for that matter. The performance was summed up for me by the statistics I read later provided by the Carling Opta Index. Phil Neville was playing as left-wingback that night, and next to his name appeared the information 'Passes successfully completed with the left foot: 0 (zero)'. Says it all, really. Poor Phil Neville. More of him later.

So, I didn't travel to Stockholm or Luxembourg. I wasn't one of the stalwarts that braved the Eastern European delights of Poland or Bulgaria. But I did do plenty of Euro 2000-related travelling before the finals themselves. I travelled to Eindhoven. Then I went to Amsterdam. And Eindhoven, and Charleroi, and Brussels. Then I went to Rotterdam. Then to Brussels. Then there was a trip to Arnhem and Eindhoven. Then I went to Amsterdam, and Deventer, and even Dusseldorf. Then I went to Brussels. And after that of course, I travelled to Euro 2000.

My untypical Euro 2000 experience came about because I was employed as co-ordinator of the Football Supporters' Association's Fans' Embassy. Fan's embassies are a good idea; basically, an advice and information service for travelling supporters, which over the years has grown into a means of speaking up for football supporters and generalising their experiences and interests to an often hostile media.

Some of the tournament experiences I shared with all the other England fans. I watched the same games, as many as possible from inside the grounds. I saw the same Phil Neville, unfortunately. I ate and drank in many of the same bars and restaurants. But there were differences. As a result of working full-time at the Embassy, I talked to hundreds, if not thousands of other fans. Team meetings with the embassy volunteers gave me the benefit of their contact with thousands of supporters, in towns hosting games and elsewhere. I also had access to, and meetings with, police chiefs, town mayors and officials, community leaders, FA representatives, consular officials, and fan co-ordinators of all participating countries. In all modesty, I think I had as detailed and as rounded-out a view of what went on at the tournament as any other individual.

But I hardly recognised the picture painted by the press reports I read. Certainly the average person at home, watching the tournament from afar, on television or through the press, would not think to question the implication that English football fans were not welcome. They'd seen the pictures, heard the reports, and who could blame the citizens of Charleroi for being impatient to see the back of the English after all that? They'd been caught up in a war zone, hadn't they, their town centre transformed into a battlefield for days on end by masses of hooligans. OK, not every England fan was like that, but most of them must be – after all, nearly a thousand had been arrested. Charleroi now needed time to recover, didn't it? Charles Bremner of *The Times* clearly thought so; his article on the leaving of Charleroi was entitled *English Leave Bad Taste For Battered Residents.*

This view of what had happened in Charleroi had now spread across the entire continent. The whole of Europe's media seemed to be peddling the same version of events – and drawing similar conclusions. The Dutch paper *Trouw* had an answer: 'There's only one thing left, and that's to ban the England team from large European tournaments.'

Brussels's French language newspaper *La Derniere Heure* said that the threat to suspend the England team from Euro 2000 was not enough, and instead wanted an outright ban on all English clubs and teams.

Even the Swiss wanted to get in on the act. Never mind the fact that they hadn't qualified and weren't even here – that didn't stop the *Basler Zeitung* abandoning any thought of neutrality. According to them, 'the Charleroi police were just happy that their town had not been laid waste.'

This sort of press coverage was not a new arrival on the Euro 2000 scene. The media had begun predicting trouble in Charleroi as soon as the draw was made that placed the England v Germany encounter in the small Wallonian town. All the usual tabloid suspects were involved, but the hype became so intense that even some people of whom I had come to expect more got caught up in it and felt moved to add their own contribution.

The Observer's Denis Campbell, for instance. On the 4th June, he wrote:

> *An Observer investigation reveals that Charleroi is set to be turned into a battlefield with visiting thugs, local Turks and neo-Nazi troublemakers based in the town staging bloody confrontations. The authorities privately admit mayhem is almost guaranteed because huge numbers of mainly ticketless fans will crowd into Charleroi's narrow streets.*

On the same day, Andrew Longmore was writing in the *Independent on Sunday*, in a slightly more measured article headlined *What Did They Do To Deserve Us?*

> *Whoever redesigned modern Charleroi must have known something. Tucked into the north-eastern corner of this unpretentious – some might say deeply unlovely – Belgian town lies a complex of buildings which will become the focal point of activity, one way or another, on the night of 17th June. On one side of Boulevard Zoe Drion is the Stade du Pays de Charleroi . . . across the road is the city hospital, a block away the Palais de Justice and, straddling the two, the essential link in the evolutionary cycle of the English football hooligan, the home of the local* gendarmerie. *Pinched, imprisoned and prosecuted, all within half-a-square mile. Who said the Belgians were unprepared?*

All this talk of impending doom began before long to smell like a self-fulfilling prophecy. If enough column inches are filled predicting the hooligan equivalent of World War Three breaking out on the streets of Charleroi, then before long it becomes *the* place, on *the* weekend, where every self-respecting hooligan (well, no-one else is likely to respect them) throughout Europe has to be.

None of the media coverage of the prospective battles allowed the story to be spoilt by the intrusion of the fact that there has not been any particular history of trouble at England-Germany games. Despite the fact that the Euro '96 game between the two countries took place in London and at the high-pressure semi-final stage, there were no significant incidents reported. Nor even in the otherwise problematic Italia '90 World Cup.

You would have thought though, wouldn't you, that the many sponsors of the tournament and of its competing teams would have been striving behind the scenes to play down all this talk of problems. They would seem to have a vested interest in a trouble-free event as a backdrop for the highlighting of the products and services they were seeking to sell us. Well, you'd have thought so, but even *they* weren't always immune from the frenzy of foreboding.

One particularly overblown article on the subject of the fate about to befall Charleroi – I say 'about to', but this article actually appeared in January 2000 – reported that the town's inhabitants were 'not looking forward to seeing us'. It revealed that 'a staggering 1,100 police officers will be on duty for the meeting of the old arch-rivals, in an attempt to ward off potential problems.' It then quotes the former Sporting Charleroi programme editor (now there's an authoritative source!) as saying 'It's a big problem and there has been a feeling of fear since the draw was made. We hope the police are up to the job.'

The article went on to relate that the top tier of the three-tiered stand in the stadium was to be removed after the tournament, though 'one high-ranking town official, it is rumoured, has stated his fears that English and German hooligans may do the dismantling job for them.' This cheery piece of reporting of the latest 'rumours' ended for the sake of balance with a reference to 'the legacy of Heysel'.

The sort of article that would have team sponsors threatening to withdraw advertising from the publication irresponsible enough to print it, you would have thought. Well, yes, except that this particular (unsigned) article could be read, apparently exclusively, on the website of Nationwide, official sponsors to Team England.

That was the general tenor of the material that appeared in the press in advance of the tournament. There was of course the predictable article in every tabloid about how their own undercover reporter had been able to travel to Charleroi and, after only half-an-hour in the town, track down and buy black market tickets for the game. These articles are usually followed by an opinion piece, which funnily enough almost always misses the obvious conclusion, of suggesting a ticketing system that puts the tickets into the hands of the real supporters in the first place. Instead the editorials usually call for evermore-draconian measures to be taken not against the UEFA bureaucrats who thought up the system in the first place, but against any poor fan who tries to get into the game this way.

(It strikes me too that if I were a tout in the town where a tournament is to be held, I wouldn't hold on to sell my ticket until match day, when there's likely to be a lot more police attention. I'd get rid of it three months in advance, when some tabloid hack with an expense account will pay top dollar for it to give himself an 'exclusive'.)

The next round of 'exclusives' in every tabloid before every tournament is always the expose of the thugs who will run riot before the game. As often as not, these 'exclusives' uncovered by intrepid investigative journalists – who are usually referred to in their by-lines as 'crime correspondents' – are in fact rehashed versions of scaremongering press releases sent out by the football unit of the National Criminal Intelligence Service, or NCIS.

One particularly fine example of this genre appeared in the *Sunday Mirror* of June 4th. That day, the *Sunday Mirror* seemed to be suffering from a split personality. It published its 8-page Euro 2000 pull-out guide, which apart from being a bit heavy on the advertising for Burton Menswear, the official menswear supplier to the England football team, was very good. This section was backed up by the sports pages, which carried more very good stuff previewing the tournament, quite balanced, just enough optimism to keep the spirits up without getting carried away. And even better, there was Brian McNally's *Fanzone* column taking up problems with UEFA's ticketing system and the imbalanced number of tickets it gave to sponsors, corporate clients and civic dignitaries.

Sadly for *Sunday Mirror* readers, the other, darker side of the paper's personality was manifested in the news pages. Replacing the strapline used at the top of all the sports pages, which read *Euro 2000 Countdown*, page 31 had instead *Euro 2000 – Countdown To Another Nightmare* above its headline of *The Thugs Army*. Sure enough, there in the article, (after the sober introduction 'An Army of 1,000 football yobs is heading for the Euro 2000 tournament hellbent on bloodshed, the Sunday Mirror can reveal today . . .'), is a quote from its source, one Brian Drew of NCIS, who provides the figure of one thousand hooligans. Presumably the 'exclusive' part of the article is where Crime Correspondent Tim Luckett comes up with the figure of 10,000 people travelling to

Eindhoven for the Portugal game. He doesn't of course reveal his source for this figure; ten thousand is a lot more than the official ticket allocation to the FA, yet to me would seem a significant underestimate of the total likely to travel. Tim then, presumably with the aid of a calculator, reveals that therefore one in ten of the fans travelling are known soccer hooligans.

The cynic in me, by the way, often wonders whether the NCIS budget for the next couple of years is determined in the March to May period before a major tournament. I have no firm evidence to back this up, no mole in their accounts department – it just sometimes seems that the flurry of figures always released by the 'service' around this time does nothing quite as effectively as justify the football intelligence unit's existence. Their press releases have become as much a regular feature of the pre-tournament build-up as the announcement that most of those actually involved in trouble around the subsequent games were unknown to them is part of the aftermath.

Then in the scramble to outdo each other, the tabloids go to greater and greater lengths. Conveniently ignoring the apologies some had had to make after Euro '96 for their xenophobic and in particular anti-German headlines, they gradually raised the temperature of the supposed Anglo-German antagonism. Eventually the pinnacle – or nadir – was reached with the story of the two separate morgues being prepared, one for English corpses, one for Germans. I couldn't help but wonder what exactly the point of this was. I had visions of zombie wars, as the undead of two nations fought over the prime fridge space, pausing only to examine each other's toe tags to check which side they were on.

The Charleroi weekend was the subject of all these traditional forms of hype in the press, and sadly most of the broadcast media got caught up in the excitement too. Charleroi also became the centre of a less typical controversy, when among others the team making BBC's *Watchdog* came up with the notion that the stadium was a death-trap.

Now, I have no particular reason to champion the cause of the Stade Mambourg. The decision to hold the game between England and Germany there was made by the luck of the draw. I am not entirely convinced that the best way to determine match venues is by random selection. My doubts were reinforced when the first round game with probably the biggest demand for tickets was scheduled to take place in one of the stadia with the smallest capacity. There would have been more committed supporters able to see what was bound, regardless of the result, to be a memorable fixture had the game been held at the Roi Baudouin stadium in Brussels, which holds twenty thousand more people.

The *Watchdog* team's intentions were probably entirely honourable, motivated by a desire to avoid a disaster. However, it didn't come across that way to the people of Charleroi. They saw it much more as a foreign television company getting involved in a row being stirred up for political reasons. Many of the locals I spoke to about this were highly suspicious of the – Brussels-based – leader of the Belgian police union, the unfortunately-named (for a man to be quoted on British television) Paul van Kerr, who was regarded as part of a conspiracy by the capital. There was a certain amount of bemusement too at the fact that all this fuss was being made about the stadium for the English coming, when it had been perfectly OK for the Belgians. The English were in danger of being perceived as considering themselves too good for Charleroi.

The Stade Mambourg had of course the same safety certificates as all the other stadia earmarked for the tournament.

Local pride was wounded again by the suggestion that the rake of the three-tier stand was too steep to be safe, despite the fact that it was less steep than the Amsterdam ArenA which everyone raved about as a state-of-the-art venue. I'm looking forward to Ann Robinson's crusade to close the San Siro and the Stade de France next both of which are steeper than Charleroi's stand.

Nonetheless, once the story got going, every newspaper had to send its own reporter to see the death-trap stand for themselves. Just about every one of them reported on the mountain rescue training given to first aid workers responsible for dealing with any medical evacuations, and they all quoted the same sources about how disastrous it would be if fighting broke out in the upper tier. There must have been more English than Belgian journalists in the press box for the Belgium v Portugal friendly held in Charleroi in the run-up to the tournament, and very few of them were there to report on Emile Mpenza.

Given that sort of build-up to the June 17th, it would have been a miracle if the weekend had passed off without trouble. The hype was like a magnet to every racist hooligan in northern Europe. The local population was on edge. I imagine that even the most levelheaded *gendarme* would have felt tense and nervous as he pulled on his jackboots that morning. And of course the media, having written the programme notes and the advance publicity, were settled in around the main square, the arena for the day's events, waiting for the action. The newsdesks were on standby, ready to receive the pictures they were expecting. The copy was in some cases possibly already written.

Very few lies were told in the reporting. There *were* racist thugs chanting vile abuse, threatening, intimidating, fighting, and they deserved all the vitriol the press poured on them. It's not false to say that there were some three thousand police involved on the day, or that hundreds of fans, most of them English were arrested. It is undeniable that water cannon were deployed after trouble broke out in the square during the day. Known hooligans were present. A lot of alcohol was drunk. Damage was done. And all of this was well documented, caught on camera and broadcast around the world and back.

The problem is that, having helped create an expectation that bad things would happen in Charleroi, and in the process probably contributing to making them worse than they need have been, the media reported these truths as if they were the only truth. With some honourable exceptions, a very one-sided picture was painted, giving a distorted impression that ceased to be the whole truth. Sadly, that one-sided perception is the one that has been fed to television audiences and newspaper readerships, and has been used to form their judgements of the whole tournament, and of all England fans. Even more dangerously, it seems also to be the perception that has shaped the thinking of lawmakers and politicians.

It is not really surprising that people receive a distorted impression without anyone telling them any lies. It's so easy, if you see fans fighting, water cannon spraying, police charging, and chairs flying on the lunch-time, mid-afternoon, early evening, nine o'clock and late evening news bulletins, to form the impression that the fighting has been going on all day. In fact, there were two incidents involving water cannon in the Place Charles II on the Saturday afternoon, and I'd be surprised if they added up to ten minutes between them. Yet the television footage of those ten minutes was broadcast around the world over and over again, accompanied by commentary on 'England's Shame'.

Of course it's dramatic television, an exciting story, and it lends itself to easy, sweeping conclusions. No wonder editors love it; two hundred people fighting is much more compulsive viewing than fifteen thousand fans sharing bars, restaurants and open spaces with German supporters, trading Klinsmann jokes rather than blows.

So how about a different version of what happened in Charleroi, a more sober assessment, one based more on the experiences of the majority?

'You see: the stand did not collapse; the town is not demolished, and no-one died. There was no more unrest than at a robust carnival.

'This tournament has contributed to the positive image of the town. There was a lot of pleasure here. The five minutes when the seats flew through the air don't alter that.

'The media stood around the Place Charles II waiting for something to happen. It was scandalous.'

This version of events above doesn't, funnily enough, come from the FSA. These words are the reflective assessment of Jacques van Gompel, Mayor of Charleroi, as given to the Belgian newspaper *De Standaard* (June 24th 2000). Even in the immediate aftermath of the Germany game, van Gompel said 'Considering what we were expecting, the level of violence was quite low. Most of the English fans behaved well and the hooligans were prevented from causing real disturbances.'

But what of the 400-plus arrests in Charleroi? Well, let's take into consideration the reflections of Colonel Herman Bliki, the man in charge of the *gendarmerie*'s Euro 2000 anti-hooligan operation. He told *The Bulletin*, an English language Brussels publication (June 29th 2000): 'Most of the arrests resulted from problems of identification. English people don't carry their passports with them, so we had to take them to the station just to identify them. There were only twenty-eight real arrests.'

There may not have been quite the same shock horror

response back home had the news from Charleroi been that there were 28 arrests, not 400. In fact, given the build-up and the expectations, an outcome of 28 arrests, no serious injuries (the one person stabbed, who was English, turned out not to be seriously hurt), and half-a-dozen broken windows could be considered a bit of an anti-climax.

But there is more reason to tell the real story of what happened at Euro 2000 than just to put the record straight, worthwhile though that would be. Much more serious is the fact that this distorted, tabloid version of events is the starting point for the lawmakers and politicians who are rushing through ill-thought legislation to combat the problems they've seen highlighted.

There are hundreds of innocent England fans who have had their Euro 2000 experience ruined by being arrested, even deported, simply for being in the wrong place at the wrong time. That nightmare could now be compounded if the police are given powers to prevent them travelling to future tournaments, adding future injustices to the ones they've already suffered. Legislation to combat hooligans, if it is to work, needs to be based on a solid foundation of an accurate assessment of what the problem is. The real story, not the version designed to sell newspapers.

Wembley To Eindhoven

Friday 9th & Saturday 10th June

FIRST DESTINATION FOR England at Euro 2000 was the city of Eindhoven.

When you're part of a Fans' Embassy though, you do things a bit differently.

You don't just head straight for Holland. Oh, no. You go to Wembley first. At six o'clock in the morning.

This wasn't just the product of some bizarre superstition based on the fact that this was the last major tournament England would play in while the historic twin towers were still standing in the borough of Brent. True, by the time of the 2002 World Cup the concrete pillars would have been demolished or, in an even crueller fate, dismantled, transported and rebuilt elsewhere by some deranged northern council desperately craving an inappropriate tourist attraction. A bit like the old Lambton Lion Park in County Durham. But probably for most England fans the schedule of 30 very last, historic, commemorative farewell-to-Wembley matches (including two FA Cup semi-finals, a final, the Charity Shield, friendly games against Argentina, Brazil and others and a World Cup qualifier against Germany) was going to be enough for them to say goodbye.

Or more likely, good riddance. It's niggled me for years that

I've had to pay dramatically increased season ticket prices to see games, all justified by the fact that football has moved on and left behind the bad old days when facilities were so poor that a visit to the toilet meant having to stand ankle deep in urine. Then your team battles its way to the FA Cup Final (or strings together five lucky wins against inferior opposition delivered by incredible luck of the draw, depending on your point of view), and this pinnacle of achievement, the game of the season, is the most expensive yet, but a visit to the toilet means having to stand ankle deep in urine. That and losing there in three consecutive seasons certainly explains Alan Shearer's nostalgic comment that the sooner they pull it down, the better.

We had Wembley Way to ourselves early that morning, funnily enough. Just half-a-dozen members of the Embassy team, two liveried vehicles and two of the public relations industry's finest. Oh, and three television camera crews, two photographers and a radio reporter. A publicity event, you understand.

Jardine PR had thoughtfully arranged for flasks of coffee and an abundance of croissants to be on hand, and to fill the time between live interviews, we set up a table and chairs. And that's how it was that passers-by on their way to work that Friday morning were confronted by the sight of eight people in identical polo shirts having a picnic early in the morning on Wembley Way, in the rain. Probably very similar in appearance to a small but well-funded religious sect conducting some open-air bread-breaking ritual before setting out on an evangelical mission into deepest Harlesden. We must have looked very odd; we certainly felt it.

Eindhoven is, in essence, Philips-town. The electronics giant has put its stamp on the city, giving rise to its nickname, the 'City of Light'. Philips employs one in five of the working population, and owns the biggest and most successful works football team in the world. The PSV in PSV Eindhoven stands for Philips Sports Club (or more accurately, Philips Sport Vereniging).

Those with the job of selling Eindhoven have made a virtue of necessity and happily admit that Eindhoven is not a town of great tradition or beauty, but grew up around hi-tech industries. 'No mediaeval history here – instead a portrait of our own era'. They have a strange idea of visitors' likely preferred reading material though; the regional tourist board's guidebook suggests 'a stroll through Eindhoven, with a history of the Philips company in your hand . . .'

PSV Eindhoven's ground – the Philips Stadium – is near the town centre, on the edge of a part of town known as 'Philips Dorp'. Go past the Philips Health Centre and it's on your right, just before you reach the Philips Reception Centre. All of which could lead you to conclude that it's all a bit corporate – and you wouldn't be wrong.

I've been to the Philips Stadium a few times now, but I still laugh every time I approach it and am confronted by the massive Toys'R'Us sign on one end. The ground floor at that end is indeed given over to a massive toyshop. And the whole of the rest of the stadium comes across as primarily dedicated to the carrying out of business, in the sort of comfort that businessmen have become accustomed to. There are overhead heaters above the ordinary seats for winter games, but executive boxes set the tone, complete with airline style seats, television screens and optional crowd noise. I attended a conference there in August 1999, organised by the Dutch Government to discuss the treatment of fans at Euro 2000. Part of the event was a tour of the ground, during which our guide felt obliged to point out that the seats in the executive lounges could, if required, swivel round to face the pitch.

All of which has contributed, no doubt, to the fact that

PSV are the most hated club in Holland. Something to do with money, apparently, and an arrogance that goes with it. I'm sure if I stopped to think about it, I could come up with an English equivalent.

The latest bid by the club to win the hearts and minds of fans of all the smaller clubs in Dutch football was a real masterstroke. It took the form of a statement of intent by the club president that he intends to quit the Dutch league in 2002 to launch a 16-club European League, along with the top teams from Portugal, Greece, Belgium, Norway and Scotland, as the Dutch First Division is 'out of date'. No doubt the lads from the *Oost Side* (the Toys'R'Us end) will be relishing the chance of those easy away trips to Celtic or Panathanaikos, or the local derby match against Bruges.

I met some canny people at PSV though, on my pre-tournament visits. Everybody was very polite and falling over themselves to be friendly and helpful. I found it hard to dislike a club that has pictures of Bobby Robson all over its corridors. It was like going to a stranger's house and discovering that he was mates with your Grandad.

The people working for the fan project there, Patrick and Nell, were both very co-operative. But I was particularly impressed by a bloke called Hans, who used to work for the fan project but who had recently started a new job as Head of Stadium Security. He spoke very highly of my Grandad – sorry, of Bobby Robson – as did everybody there. They all said Bobby was a real gentleman, and Hans told this tale of when he bumped into Bobby in the stadium one day after training. Bobby was wearing a new pair of shoes, which Hans complimented him on. So Bobby, after checking they'd fit, gave them to him. Somehow I couldn't imagine Ruud Gullit doing that.

Eindhoven is also a university town, and there are quite a lot of young people about. There's also a street called the

Stratumseind in the town centre, a pedestrianised precinct known as 'the street of a hundred bars', though I didn't count them. One bank holiday Friday I was there, the place was jumping. If I closed my eyes, I could have been in Newcastle's Bigg Market, except the people in Eindhoven probably spoke more comprehensible English. To a less enlightened, politically-correct person than me, the words 'top totty' would also have leapt to mind. Probably. Over and over again. To the extent that you'd have to lie down in a darkened room. I should imagine.

Most England fans heading for the Portugal game would stay over in or around Amsterdam, and just travel into Eindhoven on match day.

When you're part of a Fans' Embassy though, you do things a bit differently.

We went straight to Eindhoven, because we had loads of Fans' Embassy-type things to sort out. Lots of the 15-strong volunteer team hadn't been before, so they had to go and familiarise themselves with the lie of the land. Those of us who had done the pre-tournament visits got on with unloading the tools of our embassy trade from the van. We'd only just started when we were approached by the Rubenesque pulchritude of Sky News reporter Philippa Young. (I hope she likes that description, Rubenesque pulchritude. In Geordie, that would translate as something like 'She's a big lass, she's a bonny lass'. I can't confirm if, like Cushy Butterfield, she also liked her beer. But I can confirm that my mate Paul Thomas thought she was gorgeous.)

Five minutes into talking to Philippa and we were joined by a BBC camera crew. Both channels wanted interviews about what we were doing, so we duly obliged. Five minutes we'd been in town, and already two television interviews – a sign of things to come. Both interviews included the question 'Are you expecting a lot of trouble from the England fans?' – another sign of things to come, and perhaps a suggestion that they already knew the story they were looking for.

They didn't keep us long, so we could get on with the business at hand, which at this point consisted of unloading some of the 10,000 copies of the first edition of our fanzine, *The Lowdown*, ready to be distributed to England fans as they arrived.

Now, if somebody were to ask me why we produced a fanzine, my answer would probably be: who wants to know? If it was the Home Office or somebody similar asking, I'd probably answer something like 'We believe it will be an excellent means of communicating with England fans, and encourage a positive and friendly interaction with the host population and fans of other countries.'

If it was the *Sunday Mirror*, I'd say 'Your sponsorship of the fanzine is itself testimony to what a success it can be, and we are particularly pleased to have your own columnist Brian McNally contributing to it.'

If the Kick Racism Out Of Football campaign asked, I'd reply 'We believe it's vital that we can communicate a clear anti-racist message to England's travelling support, and hopefully help set the tone for how we all conduct ourselves.'

And to any England fan that asked why they should read it, I'd say 'Because it's a good laugh, you'll enjoy it, hopefully as much as we enjoyed putting it together.'

And all the answers would be true, experience having taught me that if you want to get a worthy message across, it's best to make it entertaining at the same time.

We'd really enjoyed compiling and writing the fanzine, and it was a genuine team effort. And while I don't like singling out any one individual for attention, I'm going to anyway. We were fortunate to be able to call on the services of Phil

Rowley, Scouse wit and trivia connoisseur. He provided us with most of the questions for our *Lowdown* Good-for-Nothing Quiz on football trivia, but during the course of one of our pre-tournament visits, he'd also revealed a frightening knowledge of eighties pop music. There was nothing he couldn't recall; anything you'd ever wanted to know about those kitsch one-hit wonders, and a lot more you didn't. One evening when we'd been reconnoitring (ahem!) the bars of Amsterdam, Phil had kept up a barrage of quiz questions all night, to our great amusement and well beyond, all of it unaffected by the alcohol we were all consuming. In fact he could still formulate trivia questions when the rest of us could no longer formulate words. A remarkable achievement, until it dawned on us that was *all* he could actually manage. Even that fact didn't become clear until two of the team greeted him cheerily the next morning and Phil, whisky bottle still in hand, replied 'Who sang "Love is a Wonderful Colour"?'

Phil almost met his match later that day. We had completed a tour of the Philips Stadium and were sitting down to lunch with a young man in a suit by the name of Oliver, who was representing the Euro 2000 Foundation. Oliver was treating us to a lengthy and detailed discourse on all the arrangements for the England v Portugal game he was so pleased to be hosting, and he didn't spare us a single detail. So thorough was he that when he'd finished talking and asked if we had any questions, there was an uneasy silence as we tried to think of an issue he hadn't already dealt with. Phil found one. 'I've got a question: who sang "Life is Life"?' Oliver didn't bat an eyelid. Absolutely deadpan, he replied 'Opus. Any more questions?'

Phil saw off the challenge however. Oliver did know that 'Always There' was a hit for Incognito, but he very apologetically admitted he didn't know who had sung 'Einstein A Go-Go'. (It was, of course, Landscape.)

Phil Rowley haunted me for a week or two after that. Not particularly because of the gaps in my knowledge about The Icicle Works; much more because a television interview I did in Amsterdam appeared with the caption 'Phil Rowley of the Football Supporters' Association'. The bar we watched it in was full of Dutchmen who, pointing at me, broke into a chant of 'Rowley, Rowley!', pronounced as in 'Roly Poly'. Disconcerting enough any way, doubly so when you're my shape. For days I wandered around Holland convinced Dutch people were whispering to each other 'There's Rowley, the rotund England fan!'

That football quiz in full (answers p.228):

The Lowdown Good-For-Nothing Quiz

1 Who are the 3 former England internationals with 3 'O's in their surnames?

2 Six players with an 'X' in their surnames have been capped by England since 1982. Who are they?

3 Only 5 players scored for England in the Euro 2000 qualifying campaign. Who are they?

4 Which former England international played in Manchester, North London, Merseyside and North East derbies between 1988 and 1997?

5 What prevented Pele from joining Real Madrid after the 1958 World Cup Final?

6 In the 1999–2000 season in the league, Arsenal did it 17 times, Man. Utd 13 times, and Wimbledon only twice. What was it?

7 The name of which English club begins with 5 consonants?

8 At the start of last season, what did Everton's Richard Dunne have more of than anyone else in the Premiership?

9 Which English league club has never played in its home town?

10 Which one team in the Premiership last season has most shots off target (281), corners (277) and committed the most fouls (626)?

11 Which Premiership player said: 'Whenever I play in London I get Seaman rammed down my throat'?

12 Who was the last team to play in stripes to win the FA Cup Final?

The quiz wasn't the only intellectually taxing part of the fanzine. We'd also compiled a Wordsearch, of the type so popular with nine-year-olds and pensioners on coach trips. Hidden in our grid of letters were several words that broadly fell under the heading of 'Dutch'. They broke down into three categories. First, those whom nobody could deny were associated in the popular consciousness with Holland – such as windmill, Van Gogh, dyke, clog, Edam, Gouda, tulips, *Oranjeboom*, Heineken, and canal.

Then there was a number more directly connected to Dutch football or the forthcoming game: Eindhoven, Philips, Gullit, De Goey, Cruyff, and Jonk.

The final category were words which might be said to relate more to – er, how can I put this? – to one of Amsterdam's tourist attractions that drew so many Euro 2000 fans towards it, the red light district. Words like dope, grass, prostitute, pimp, hash, weed, and pusher. I'm not convinced the third category will win us many awards from the Amsterdam tourist office for services rendered, but we did think it added much-needed gritty social realism.

One article in the fanzine starts to look spookily prescient in the light of later events. It took the form of a spoof press report of government plans to crack down on football hooligans:

> *The Government last night unveiled a tough new anti-hooligan policy, their third this month. This radical new policy involves 'known' troublemakers being detained in remote camps throughout East Anglia, where they will be kept busy with a programme of vigorous marching and sedative-sweetened tea. 'We are calling this new policy "National service"', said minister Lord Sea Bass. 'Detaining all young men aged 16–40 for the duration of Euro 2000 will almost certainly ensure a trouble-free tournament.' This follows shocking scenes of violence in Colchester between rival gangs armed with plastic patio furniture. 'We know who many of these hooligans are, it's just that they're so darned clever that we can't ever catch them', said a spokesman for the Non-Intelligent Criminal Service (NICS). 'Taking everyone's passports away will definitely help . . .'*

Uncomfortably near the mark, given the post-tournament proposals for the new Football Disorder Bill. I just hope we didn't give them any ideas. We do know that Government officials read the fanzine though. How? Because when one departmental official approached us to arrange a time to meet Home Office Minister Lord Bassam, he smirkingly referred to him as 'Lord Sea Bass'.

The one advantage of being in Eindhoven on the first day of Euro 2000 was that I wasn't in Brussels for the opening ceremony. Opening ceremonies scare me.

Arnhem

Sunday 11th June

I WENT TO Arnhem on the Sunday. Italy were playing Turkey in the second game of Group B, the only two-thirty kick-off of the whole tournament. It was hot, very hot, and the Turks and the Italians all seemed to be coping with the heat better than this overweight Geordie.

Four of us drove to Arnhem, two with tickets, two without. I'd hoped that I might be able to pick up a ticket or two when we got there, but demand had already outstripped supply by the time we arrived, or at least that's what the absence of any on sale on the streets in the city centre suggested. It wasn't the end of the world though; Arnhem was also the only one out of all the host cities to be boasting an outdoor giant screen. We found it without difficulty; all we had to do was follow the crowds, as the local Turkish and Italian communities had turned out in numbers for the game. The Turks formed a clear majority of the crowd in the square beside the church where the screen was, and were patiently enduring the efforts of an extremely poor local rock band on an adjacent stage.

In all the towns hosting games at big tournaments I've ever been to, there has nearly always been something that could loosely be described as musical entertainment provided at the big screen venue. They have also nearly always been dreadful. I have never yet had a conversation with anyone who has watched a match on a big screen who has felt moved to say, 'Hey, the band was great. The game was a little bit disappointing, with the defences on top and the ball getting bogged down in the overcrowded midfield, but the pre-match music more than made up for it.'

How on earth do they find 'musicians' who are so consistently awful? Presumably there is some sort of auditioning body which sifts through the applicants to find groups that are suitable. It must be a sub-committee of the organisation responsible for opening ceremonies.

There was another reason I wanted to be there. I'd been plagued by media enquiries all the previous day asking if I'd heard the rumours about the battles planned for Arnhem. Apparently the English fans were all due to descend on the town looking for confrontation with the Turks, seeking revenge for events in Istanbul. Conspiracy theories abounded; some people had Dutch hooligan groups linking up with the English to start a race war, others said it would be Germans. I was sceptical, as were the Dutch fan coaches locally, but I'd told them we would come over and see for ourselves.

Even on the way there, we were getting phone calls telling us of reports of a trainload of English fans heading for Arnhem from Eindhoven. Again I was dubious, as I'd just come from Eindhoven and I didn't think there were enough English there to fill a train. By the time we arrived, the Eindhoven express had already been met by a sizeable contingent of armed police with dogs on the look out for English-speaking hoodlums. The nearest they found was a group of six bemused Canadian war veterans and their pensioner wives, who'd arrived to re-visit the bridges. Still, better not to take any chances; they'd probably been pretty violent last time they'd been here, and they could have cut up rough if the Turks had sneaked a win.

Maybe next time the authorities in Ottawa should be a little bit more pro-active and seize the passports of known fighters like these as a precautionary measure.

I'd been to a match in Arnhem before. Only a few weeks before actually, and there had been far less panic about the hundreds, even thousands of British football fans descending on the city then than there was today. Maybe that had something to do with the fact that then the supporters were the loveable Jocks, in town for the game between Holland and Scotland. As a result of the play-off defeat at the hands of Keegan's boys, that friendly game was as near to Euro 2000 as the Scots were going to get, and they made the most of what would otherwise have been a low-key occasion. The KNVB (Dutch FA) weren't putting great store by the game; only 5,000 tickets for the game had gone on general sale, the rest being distributed to and via sponsors. All this meant that there were a disproportionate number of suits among the Dutch fans.

Not that that deterred the Jocks, who turned up mob-handed anyway. Aware of the great responsibilities towards their nation, of its history and deep-rooted traditions, thousands of supporters had arrived ready to maintain their cultural heritage. To the uncultured outsider this heritage appeared to involve wearing skirts and drinking to oblivion. England fans are all too aware that our tradition appears to the uncultured outsider (or tabloid journalist) to involve wearing no shirts, big boots, drinking to oblivion and throwing things at foreigners.

The image of Scottish football fans has been the subject of a makeover that would upstage the *Changing Rooms Christmas Special*. It's not that long ago that the thought of thousands of rampaging Jocks descending on a foreign city filled the locals with dread. In European club football in the seventies,

Rangers fans were numbered among the worst offenders for hooliganism on foreign soil. Not necessarily that foreign either. Older Newcastle fans still reminisce like octogenarian war veterans about the day in 1969 when Rangers hit town for a Fairs Cup semi-final, second leg. To hear the story retold, at least 50,000 of the 59,303 crowd were stabbed or at least robbed at knife point by marauding Glaswegians. Also, schoolchildren today refuse to believe that when the crossbar was snapped in a pitch invasion at Wembley in 1977 after an England–Scotland game, those loveable Caledonian rascals could have had anything to do with it.

Nowadays the Scots are, quite rightly, universally loved and welcomed. Not least by the local representatives of the host nation's equivalent of the Licensed Victuallers' Association. Sure, they're often drunk. Certainly, they're usually noisy, in a gruff, off-key, enthusiastic, incomprehensible but most probably patriotic way. But they're never any trouble. The time and effort spent clearing up after them is seldom begrudged, the overtime for the street cleaners being a rare example of the much-vaunted 'trickle-down' effect of wealth distribution.

Perhaps the most remarkable aspect of this change in the perception of Scottish football fans abroad is that nobody can quite explain how or when this change came about. I'd like to congratulate the Scottish FA on their highly effective campaign to promote a positive image across the world, but I'm not actually aware of one. A wise Scottish friend of mine puts it down to the nation coming to the conclusion that they were never likely to win anything, so they may as well have a laugh. I'm not so sure. Fielding a team that more often than not inspires more sympathy than admiration doesn't quite explain it; if that was a decisive factor, then Millwall fans would be accorded a significantly warmer welcome on their travels than they currently enjoy. Was it then an imperceptibly gradual accumulation of See-You-Jimmy wigs that infected Scots fans with good humour?

Whatever it has been that's effected such a change, England's support could use some. If they could bottle it they'd make a fortune. Though if it came in bottles, chances are there wouldn't be much of it left when the Scots had had all they wanted. Then again, there are always some arseholes attached to England's support that'd find a use for the empties.

My first encounter with the massed ranks of the Tartan Army abroad was in Paris for the opening game of the 1998 World Cup. I remember wondering at the volume, in both senses of the word, of Scottish fans there when the thought crossed my mind that there couldn't be many June weddings taking place in Scotland that summer. Not simply because of the number of Scotsmen who were clearly out of the country; numerous though they were, they didn't constitute 49% of the Scottish population. It was the number of kilts on display. My brother was due to be married that September in Dumbarton, so I'd had a brief insight into what exactly was involved. I could clearly envisage the exchanges taking place in wedding hire shops across Scotland that spring: 'I'm awfully sorry, sir, we can kit out your wee page boy no problem, but we've no adult size kilts in the McLeod or any other tartan available until after the group stage.'

In my experience, Scots only wear kilts at weddings and away international matches. There aren't many worn for shopping expeditions down Sauchiehall Street, but in Paris there were Scotsmen everywhere, and almost without exception they wore kilts. In fact the rare Scotsman in jeans or trousers was greeted with the raised eyebrows and muttered disapproval more usually reserved for . . . well, for blokes wearing skirts as much as anything. (Oh sorry, Mr Beckham, it's a *sarong*, is it?)

As if to substantiate this theory about kilts being exclusively worn at weddings and international matches, one of the first acts of practical assistance we had been able to provide in France was to relieve one Scotland fan of his skean dhu, which he'd unexpectedly found in his sporran. 'It must have been in there since the last wedding I was at', he explained. He'd realised that daggers, ceremonial or otherwise, would probably fall into one of the categories of objects not welcome in World Cup football stadia. We'd agreed to look after it for him in order he could enter the Stade de France unhindered, and were pleased to be able to return it to him only four-and-a half months later.

Another observation struck me: the Scots fans seem largely to have travelled in groups of twelve. It transpired that was not some relic of the clan system, but a symptom of a much more modern, not exclusively Highland phenomenon, the minibus. Even though in some cases the minibus was only used to ferry the group to Prestwick Airport. I had conducted a random but methodologically totally unscientific survey of these groups, and a distinct trend began to emerge. Of these groups of twelve, usually one of them, often referred to as 'the big man', had a match ticket. (There is no conclusive evidence to suggest a direct link between ownership of the ticket and the size of the man.) The other eleven were his 'pals', who'd just come along for the party, to have a drink in Paris, meet some Brazilians, and who'd find somewhere to watch the match on a telly.

Naturally, not all the Scots travelled in dozens. Most of those who didn't were a different breed altogether. Travelling in threes, they too wore kilts, but instead of wearing them appropriately with a replica Scotland top, they wore frilly white shirts and bow ties. These people became known as 'posh Jocks', although strangely they didn't have Scottish accents. They had discovered Scottish ancestry as soon as they heard that the merchant bank they worked for had acquired three tickets for the Brazil game, and had been looking forward to supporting those brave laddies in blue ('It is blue they wear, isn't it?') ever since. Funnily enough, they did not seem to mix with the other Scots fans; it didn't seem appropriate after they'd arrived in Paris on the same Eurostar train as Richard Branson and his entourage.

There hadn't been many posh Jocks in Arnhem. Meaningless midweek friendlies abroad are strictly the preserve of the dedicated supporter, not the corporate freeloader. The Scots who did make the trip had a great time, though it was despite rather than because of the match, a dismal nil-nil draw, played at walking pace. You got the feeling that the biggest concern was to avoid picking up injuries for the big games ahead, rather than seizing the chance to impress Frank Rijkaard before he made his final squad selection. At least that would explain the Dutch lethargy; it's a bit harder to believe that Neil McCann was saving himself in case he got a last-minute call up to the Dutch Euro 2000 squad.

The Scots fans sang continuously, but without really being able to generate much atmosphere, perhaps because the hardcore of their support was boxed in behind big reinforced Perspex screens in the area usually reserved for the away fans visiting Vitesse Arnhem. For some reason, their repertoire of songs seemed to include a large number about hating the English, which seemed to me to have no more relevance to a game against the Dutch than England fans voicing their refusal to surrender to the IRA ever has to do with the games their team is involved in.

The Holland v Scotland game in Arnhem was one of the

most dreadful games I've ever been to. The atmosphere was not threatening or unpleasant, it was non-existent, and most of that problem can be put down to the stadium itself. I think it's horrible.

Yet the Gelredome is a state-of-the-art stadium, supposedly the model for the future. Coventry City's new stadium is said to be being based on the same sort of design. German Bundesliga club Schalke 04's new ground, *Auf Schalke*, is also modelled on the same concept, though much bigger (61,000 capacity instead of 30,000, and with 16,000 of those places on standing terraces).

Maybe I've formed my opinion based on a distorted impression. It was a dull, meaningless game after all, played before far too many corporate clients that even the Jocks couldn't stir into life. But the event had the feel of a basketball game, and a lot of the blame for that must lie with the fact that the roof was kept closed throughout the match. Well, not quite throughout; it was opened at half-time to let the smoke out. Honest.

The stadium has all the modern amenities you would expect – from a cinema complex. Bars, souvenir shops, various sorts of food counters, ice cream parlours, loads of places for you to spend your money. Well, not money exactly, because none of the retail outlets in the Gelredome will accept your money, even if you've gone to all the trouble of changing your Scottish pounds into Dutch guilders. Not easy, given that you will have had to convince the staff at the Bureau de Change that the Clydesdale Bank is a real financial institution legally entitled to produce its own banknotes rather than the subsidiary of the Bank of Toyland that boasts McNoddy as its most famous customer.

The Gelredome deals only in a currency known as the Ohra, named, surprise surprise, after a sponsor. Before the numismatists reading this (and there are clearly bound to be many) get all excited about the prospect of a new range to add to their collection, I should point out that this currency has neither coins nor notes. Its units (Ohras) are stored on plastic cards. Around the stadium are conversion machines where you can insert your guilders (or even more perversely, your plastic cards) and buy yourself a card full of Ohras. Now you're all tooled up, and you can go and purchase your snack or whatever.

What you can't do is get any change, however. So if you don't spend all your Ohras, the unspent ones remain on your card. This may not be the end of the world if you're a Vitesse season ticket holder and will be back in a fortnight's time. Even then, it would still be a bit of a pain in the arse, and of course in the meantime the Gelredome is sitting on your real money, earning interest on it or whatever, in a form of compulsory savings scheme. But it's not much cop if you've just arrived from Easterhouse or Istanbul, and by the time your team plays here again, if ever, Vitesse will probably have whole new sponsor and a whole new currency to match.

Or if, as is just as likely in an 'arena' like this, you've come for the Backstreet Boys concert, since by the time they come back to Arnhem – if they last that long – you'll have grown out of them and be married with kids of your own who will have long since chewed your Gelredome Ohra card out of any recognisable shape.

And if you have a raging thirst on the way out of the ground and you decide to use up the balance of your Ohras on buying one last Coke, you can guarantee that the spotty adolescent press-ganged into underpaid service behind the counter will tell you that you're one poxy Ohra short of the price of their smallest beaker, and will refuse to dispense a short measure to match your shortage of virtual funds, because it's all computerised and the system doesn't allow for that sort of convenient flexibility. Said youth will then suggest, in terms so polite that you feel guilty for losing your temper, that the only solution is to go back to the conversion machine and recharge your Ohra card, in the full and certain knowledge that this will mean that whatever size beaker you subsequently buy, the surplus Ohras you've now acquired will make it the most expensive soft drink ever bought outside a Soho strip club. So you go home thirsty, still in possession of a piece of plastic containing six bloody Ohras, and you try to overcome your rage by doing something magnanimous like giving your card to some underprivileged-looking kid who may one day save up enough of his meagre pocket money to afford to return to another football match. But all you can see around you are smug spoilt little brats weighed down with all the over-priced merchandise Daddy's abundant Ohras could buy, walking hand-in-hand with their bourgeois parents who've just concluded a great business deal at their first ever soccer match that their boss has insisted they come to, but at least they entered into the spirit of it and wore an inflatable orange plastic crown and blew on a kazoo and brought the kids because it'll make a nice change for them, and it's the sort of thing everybody should do once.

I don't like the Gelredome.

There are all sorts of interesting things about the stadium, which may be enough to endear it to other people (not me, I'm too far gone). There's a modern fable, a sort of urban myth that the chairman of Vitesse Arnhem, one Karel Aalbers, was musing over the design for the new stadium. The drawings, so the story goes, already contained the sliding roof which had proved so successful in creating a multi-purpose stadium in the Amsterdam ArenA. But what to do about the problem of the pitch getting the rain and sunlight it needed? – the ArenA has famously had to have its pitch relaid some 15 times in four years. Mr. Aalbers took out one of his favourite cigars, reached for a match to light it and Eureka! As he slid out the tray of matches, he had the answer. And so, the pitch at the Gelredome was laid on an 11,000 tonne concrete slab designed to slide along steel strips so that it could be stored outside in the open air, and rolled into the stadium for matches. And the place was so environmentally-friendly in its construction – powered by hydro-electric motors, with further energy coming from solar panels, and all the seats were made from recycled plastic, much of it coming from old garden furniture donated by fans.

If there was an old maxim that you can always judge a town by its stadium, I'd be launching a campaign to get it changed. But there's not. I do like Arnhem though. The old town centre has a network of narrow streets with a couple of small squares, all full of bars and restaurants.

Italy won a lot more comfortably than the 2–1 scoreline suggests, I thought, and I was very impressed with Del Piero when he came on for the last 15 minutes or so. I remember thinking at the time, that lad might have a tournament he'll never forget. I watched the game in a quiet bar; the atmosphere at the big screen was lively and friendly, but it was too bloody hot. There were a few English fans in the ground and in the town, but not many, and certainly no sign of the invading armies the media had been alerting me to.

After the match, all sets of supporters mixed happily and noisily in the town, with the Italians understandably the more chirpy, before settling down for the back-to-back televised Group D games of France v Denmark and Holland v the Czech Republic. I thought Amsterdam might be the place to be for a lively night out, so we hit the road.

Amsterdam

Sunday 11th & Monday 12th June

AMSTERDAM *WAS* LIVELY on that Saturday night. There were fans there from just about all the competing nations, and quite a few as well from countries who hadn't made the cut. They just wanted to be part of the party.

There were, unsurprisingly, big numbers of Dutch fans around. There were a lot of Czechs too, more than I had expected. There were quite a few Danes, who by the time we arrived in Amsterdam had already seen their team spanked by France. They hadn't had time to be at the game itself and have returned from Bruges, so they must have endured the match in the bars of Amsterdam, which would explain their condition. Presumably they'd been drinking to forget. Their team was to go on to be dumped out of the tournament without a single point, without even scoring a single goal. Ten minutes to go in the first game, and their first choice striker Jon Dahl Tomasson was replaced, in a late attempt to unlock the French defence, by substitute Mikkel Beck. With that sort of weakness in depth, they were never likely to feature high in the top scorers list.

There were a lot of English lads about – I bumped into two sets of Geordies I knew who were there on separate stag weekends, unconnected to the football. And I also saw

Romanians, Belgians, French, Italians, Norwegians, Spanish, a few Portuguese, some Swedes – all quite happily milling around the streets, sitting outside or in bars, occasionally bursting into song. It was a snapshot of an international tournament worthy of inclusion in the next brochure. Just how it was meant to be.

All over Amsterdam, and no doubt elsewhere too, a strange ritual was being acted out, that of Meeting Foreign Fans. An unscripted but remarkably constant exchange would take place.

First, an acknowledgement or greeting. For this any language will do, but in practice it is usually English or one's own native tongue if different. So, frequently any one of: 'Hello; *Bonjour*; *Hola!*; All right mate?'

Next comes the stage of ascertaining which nationality of fan one is speaking to. This is done by naming a country in an enquiring tone of voice. The country is not chosen entirely at random, as there is certain kudos to be gained by guessing correctly. There are often useful clues that the trained eye can detect. People who would not look out of place in an early Tango advert are almost invariably Dutch. Peeling, lobster-red skin is on many occasions a distinguishing feature of the English fan, though the Cross of St. George flag draped around the shoulders can provide handy confirmation. The Danes often helpfully wear hats with Viking-style horns. Somewhat less helpfully, so do the Norwegians (I didn't say this was foolproof).

Even fans of non-qualifying countries sometimes furnished aids to identification. People who look like they have dressed themselves in tablecloths from a cheap pizzeria are probably Croatian fans. You'll also find that tartan bunnets, orange wigs and kilts are a dead give-away for a Scot. The growing popularity of face paints – don't ask me why they're growing in popularity; as far as I'm concerned they should be restricted by law to the under-eights – means that fans of other, more obscure footballing nations can also join in this ritual. They often oblige by having the name of their national team written on their forehead, or perhaps an impression of their national flag drawn on each cheek.

Please note that I can't help you when it comes to Belgians. Belgian football fans have no distinguishing features. Don't even be tempted to rely on the flag on the cheekbone – you could be looking at a German from the wrong angle, which is never a good idea.

One other rule of thumb I picked up from France '98 – beware of green-and-yellow red herrings. Experience taught me that fans with faces painted in these colours, wearing replica shirts and carrying small paper Brazilian flags on sticks were unlikely to be Brazilian. They were probably either children, wealthy tourists of American or Japanese origin, or would have begun being 'football fans' within the last fortnight. Their favourite player would be Ronaldo, who would also be the only player they could name, and they would be 100% behind him and his team, Nike. With these people, it was not worth proceeding to the next stage, and if you had already made the mistake of completing stages one and two with them, they would now be looking at you with a quizzical, slightly nervous expression. The younger ones among them would have started to cry.

Not that there were many Brazilians in Amsterdam for Euro 2000. But a similar phenomenon did begin to develop, albeit on a smaller scale – for Brazil substitute France, for Ronaldo substitute Zidane, and you get the picture.

Anyway, having ventured the name of a country, a response will be forthcoming, which will take the form of confirmation by vigorous nodding, the repetition of the name of the country, or perhaps even loud cheering, or correction by the naming of the true land of origin. This was fairly straightforward this summer, in the context of an all-European tournament, but at World Cups the process can break down at this stage. For example, I don't know what the South Korean for South Korea is, but it doesn't sound like South Korea, so it is possible to be left none the wiser. Stage two part two then takes place, reciprocating the process of national identification.

Stage three is the most important part, when the bonding takes place. Having clarified which country's fan is being addressed, status as a fellow fan is established by naming one or two key players from that country's squad. These can be selected by being their most famous player, or in some cases the only ones ever heard of beyond their own shores. Experts can develop a more refined technique, of naming players from that country who have played their league football in your domestic league. These need not necessarily have been selected for the national squad, as long as they are well known at home – such as Ginola or Di Canio. The absolute pinnacle of achievement at this stage is reached when a star member of the foreign fan's national team plays or has played his club football at your club. I found at the World Cup that this can conceivably lead to affectionate physical embraces, for example in the case of Tino Asprilla. This is less likely in cases such as Jon Dahl Tomasson.

So, typical conversations might run:

"All right, mate? Sweden? Ah, Freddy Ljungberg!"

Or:

"*Bonjour*! France? Didier Deschamps, Marcel Desailly, Frank Leboeuf!"

Or even:

"Hello! Belgium? Branko Strupar!"

*   *   *

Not all of these exchanges are guaranteed success, but one can only do one's best. In cases of difficulty, naming a high-profile club side from the appropriate country can be an acceptable substitute, if a player doesn't spring to mind. As in:

"Hello. Norway? Ah, Rosenborg!"

Guessing to conceal gaps in an otherwise encyclopaedic knowledge can work, but it's a high-risk strategy. For example, in the case of Yugoslavia, one might get away with mumbling something with -ic on the end. Similarly, most Bulgarian players seem to have names ending in -ov. But avoid risks of diplomatic incidents or fatwas. If in doubt, say something sympathetic in a friendly tone, and with a smile, and it should serve its purpose.

"Good morning. Slovenia? That's nice."

(Anyone heard uttering the phrase "Good morning. Slovenia? Ah, Edi Bajrektarevic!" would quite rightly be denounced as a flash bastard.)

In the first few days of the tournament, England fans tended to be greeted with:

"Hello. English? Ah, Alan Shearer!", although this very soon became "English? Ah, hooligan!"

As often as not, that was as far as the conversations go, as they've served their purpose. The bonds of international football fraternity are reinforced, further talk is superfluous. Even a brief exchange of this nature is sufficient to draw the conclusion, later reported back to one's compatriots, that 'I've just been talking to some (*insert appropriate nationality here*) blokes – they were really good lads!' Of course there are occasions when even greater efforts are made to communicate further, but these often involve either advanced inebriation or some form of sexual attraction as additional factors. In cases where drink plays a role, sometimes addresses can be exchanged, with every intention at the time of becoming future penpals; alternatively, in cases of larger amounts of alcohol being consumed, the same conversation can be repeated several times over. Where sexual attraction is involved, at some stage non-verbal communication may take over, from which point completely different rules apply, which I couldn't explain here even if I did understand them. (And if I did understand them, I wouldn't be wasting my time sitting here writing about them.)

The atmosphere in Amsterdam was overwhelmingly good-natured. Of course as soon as that word 'overwhelmingly' appears, there's a suggestion that it wasn't all such good news. And sad to say, the only unpleasantness I encountered that day in Amsterdam came from English fans.

While I'd been in Arnhem, another team of Embassy volunteers had spent the afternoon in Amsterdam distributing fanzines. They'd walked fairly extensively around the city, meeting England fans everywhere they went, encountering good spirits and good humour at every turn. But even earlier in the afternoon, they had informed us of a gathering of England fans beside the Grasshopper pub, just off the Damrak, on the edge of the red light district. They weren't there in massive numbers – maybe a couple of hundred – but they'd been drinking all day, and there was definitely a unpleasant undercurrent to the atmosphere.

Fans of other countries had begun to give the place a wide berth, as they didn't pick up a vibe that suggested friendly fraternisation. Instead there was steady chanting, and while there was nothing particular in the way of trouble, no violence, there was nothing inclusive about the singing. It was belligerent, nationalistic and racist. It didn't just risk causing offence, it was deliberately designed to.

That's not to say that everybody there was consciously setting out to provoke. Undoubtedly, there was a section of the English fans who had come to Euro 2000 deliberately and consciously looking for trouble, and we were to encounter them at close quarters a little later. But there was also a fair proportion who'd arrived at Centraal Station, walked down the Damrak, spotted a crowd of English and in the absence of any other detailed knowledge about the lie of the land, chosen to make the Grasshopper their first port of call.

A few drinks later and they fancy a bit of a sing. This is where some of the difficulties start to become apparent. What do you sing?

I know loads of songs to sing at Newcastle matches, and even at my age, I still join in more often than not, even though I'm self-conscious enough nowadays to know that I must look faintly ridiculous. There are traditional songs, such as 'The Blaydon Races'; there are songs which simply get behind the team or proclaim the presence of the fans; and there are songs which take the mickey out of, or to be honest even have a go at, other clubs and their fans. But it is extremely rare that there is anything chanted that is racist or genuinely offensive. And, if there was, then I would have nothing to do with it, and I think that most people at club level would feel the same way. There are plenty of positive ways to show your allegiance and support your team. And I think the same could be said about virtually all other clubs in Britain. For most fans at club level, racist and offensively provocative chanting are generally felt to be unacceptable, and there are plenty of alternatives.

But follow England away, and what do you sing? There are very few songs in the repertoire of England fans. The best ones are the ones that are clearly to do with football, that treat England as a football team, rather than a nation. 'Football's Coming Home' caught on really well at Euro '96, and I think that's partly because it combined the right sort of patriotism with an appealing amount of self-deprecation, and it was clearly a *football* song.

Then there are the spontaneous ones, usually tongue-in-cheek, in response to someone or something, like an incident or an event. Such as the 'We're not going home', sung after the tannoy announcement at the Germany game. Brilliant. But almost by definition, they don't make up a part of a regular repertoire; their whole appeal is that they are of the moment.

So what are you left with? There's a spectrum of them, ranging from the slightly dodgy, through the strange, past the bizarre to the outright offensive and in most civilised countries, illegal.

The borderline cases are things like 'The Great Escape'. I know people who see that as xenophobic, anti-German. I can see what they're getting at. I personally have a bit of a Germanophile streak, and I certainly don't see myself as insensitive to prejudices. But to deal successfully with the serious issues, I think you need a sense of proportion. I think you have to be a bit po-faced not to see the funny side of 'The Great Escape' being adopted as an England theme tune. Anyone taking it too literally needs to cast their minds back to the film – the success rate of the various escape attempts doesn't exactly give grounds for arrogance.

Maybe it gets a bit more marginal when it comes to *The Dam Busters* theme. I see that since Euro 2000 ended, Adam Crozier, the new head of the FA, has expressed his misgivings about thousands of English fans at Wembley singing *The Dam Busters* theme at the Germans. He has a point, but again, it really isn't the biggest issue we face. It's a joke at the Germans expense, but the Germans hardly constitute an oppressed racial group, and it's just as much a joke at the expense of the Luftwaffe when under Nazi command – not top of my list for defending. I read enough Victor comics as a boy to appreciate the cultural reference. I've no more based my real outlook on life or Germans on the views of Matt Braddock VC than on those of Alf Tupper, the Tough of the Track. Though maybe Alf shares some responsibility for my belief that fish and chips constitute healthy eating fit for an athlete.

So let's assume for the sake of argument that we have not suffered a sense of humour failure of, er, German proportions. What else is there?

Well, there's 'God Save the Queen' and 'Rule Britannia'. Now maybe it's just me, but I really do think these are bizarre songs for football fans to be singing. At least 'Rule Britannia' is a bit upbeat. But 'ruling the waves'? You what? Since when has ruling the waves had anything to do with football? Yachting maybe. It could be an appropriate chant for celebrating when the Royal Yacht wins the luxury cruise ship category gold medal at the Olympics. Even then I'd imagine the euphoria would be restricted to a fairly limited number of fans. But football? And since when has there really been a danger of Britons becoming slaves? Certainly not since the days of the Dam Busters, and that's stretching a point. No, it's crap. And how many of us would ever consider singing it about any other football team?

As for 'God Save the Queen' – oh, please. According to most surveys, it's a very small minority of the population who are practising Christians, and I'd guess that the proportion among match-going football fans – i.e., people with a life – is even smaller. So God really doesn't have much of a mandate here. Then, how many of us really want the Queen to reign over us? Are we really expected to set aside the battles fought to win the vote, to overthrow feudalism, to establish the limited form of parliamentary democracy we have now, and revert to defending the divine right of kings and queens? Of course not! So why the hell should we be expected to sing about it at football matches? And apart from anything else, it's an absolute dirge, highly unlikely to lift or inspire anybody to make that surging run up the wing. Particularly not the left wing, where it's most needed.

I'm afraid that my double standards do not stretch so far as to allow me to sing these songs at England games if I would object to them on principle everywhere else. Yet these are two of the few songs sung at England games that are officially sanctioned. 'Rule Britannia' should be kept for the historical anachronism that is the Last Night of the Proms. As for the national anthem, even people associated with the FA have started to question whether or not it's appropriate to play the anthems before games, as they have become a set-piece opportunity to display disrespect for other nations. So it's a sad state of affairs if that's one of the few songs in our repertoire that is not absolutely offensive to others.

What's left after them? 'No Surrender' is deplorable. Consciously introduced into the metaphorical songbook by far-right organisations like the National Front in the late seventies and early eighties, this song sounds even more absurd and objectionable now. No-one has ever yet been able to explain to me what refusal to surrender to the IRA has got to with the forthcoming game against Portugal, for instance. And it's not exactly kept up to date with the Irish peace process, has it?

The sad thing is that it has been absorbed into part of the culture of supporting England abroad, partly by default. It is sung abroad by people who would never dare, probably never even dream, of singing it at home. At a league match, if you hear people singing 'No Surrender', it's probably reasonable to assume some far-right influence at work. With England, sadly it's become part of the scenery. I remember watching that England v Argentina game in a bar in St Etienne in June 1998, where the whole pub broke into a chorus of 'No Surrender'.

(Well, not quite the whole pub, of course. I didn't.) There were two black lads just behind me joining in. I had to ask them at half-time why they'd taken part. It turned out they had no idea it was an NF-linked song, they'd just assumed it was part of following England.

And that's about it. That is about the limit of the songs regularly sung while following England. They are songs with hardly a reference to football. They're not about supporting a team, they're about flying the flag for a nation, a nation on the offensive against all other nations.

I'm not suggesting that all we need to do is learn some new songs and everything will be all right, England's fans will be as popular abroad as the Scots. But if the culture around following England is such that to take part you have no alternative presented to you other than to sink to that level, we won't be able to break the vicious circle. There needs to be a campaign at all levels to tackle the problem, and the key to winning the battle are the true supporters. A good starting point would be to encourage more positive ways of supporting the team.

Credit where it's due for the efforts that have already been made in that direction. I include among this the Sheffield Wednesday band. Now to be more frank than I should be, I've always hated bands, drums, bells, bugles and the like at football matches. Sad substitutes for real crowd atmosphere, if you ask me. And how appropriate that the band should come from Sheffield Wednesday, a club with the most woeful lack of atmosphere at its ground. But there's no denying, even by a miserable old churl like myself, that the band has played a very positive role at England games, in stirring up a bit of passion, and particularly in striking up with a different tune whenever a chorus of 'No Surrender' seemed to be swelling up. Well done.

The FA and the England Members' Club have also started to think about measures they can take to tackle this problem, which is to be welcomed. I do think though, that they need to think a bit more radically. I've been at meetings of their Euro 2000 Working Group, for example, where it was suggested, in all seriousness, that the 'No Surrender' issue should not be tackled, as it was important not to give the impression that unionists were not welcome to support England too! Surely the whole point is that the FA are about promoting Team England, a football team, and attracting around it football fans. Everybody should be welcome, and feel welcome, at football matches – providing of course that their presence doesn't make other people feel unwelcome or intimidated. And if you're there to support a football team, do you really have to bring your 'unionism' with you?

If the FA is really about generating support for a football team, maybe a bit more imagination is needed about the songs that they champion. If we're trying to break away from nationalistic songs, is the best radical alternative they can come up with for Euro 2000 really 'Jerusalem'? These people have got access to some of the most creative minds in Britain, many of whom would love to be associated with the new, modern, forward-looking FA. So what genius came up with 'And did those feet in ancient times walk upon England's mountains green . . .', by William Blake, who died 173 years ago? I'm not looking for an intellectual justification of what Blake symbolised in his day, or reminding that he refers to the 'mental fight', rather than fighting with patio furniture. All I'm saying is, there's got to be something a bit more imaginative to be part of the process of turning supporting England abroad into a positive, outgoing, friendly *football* experience.

Anyway, back to the Grasshopper. All I was trying to say, all those paragraphs ago, was that not even all those England fans who ended up outside the Grasshopper singing songs like 'No Surrender' are necessarily violent, extremist thugs consciously looking for trouble. Many of them follow whatever tone is being set. Sadly, that day, the tone was racist.

Much of the singing was famously recorded by the BBC's *Panorama* programme, which though in my opinion very one-sided certainly highlighted the problem. Nobody either can be under any illusion that chants like 'I'd rather be a Paki than a Turk' could ever be anything other than provocative.

Later that evening, I encountered some of the most unpleasant racist violence I have ever come across in connection to football. A small crew, maybe twenty or thirty, of England fans, who seemed to be from various areas but with a strong West Midlands presence, were skulking around the narrow side streets of the red-light district. A minor incident, not involving them, probably to do with petty theft, resulted in the window of an off-licence being broken. The police were on the scene within seconds, and it all seemed to blow over. A couple of minutes later, a second squad of police, perhaps responding late to the same incident, came running through the side streets. The England fans ran after them, scenting trouble. Out of the doorways of various bars en route came more, attracted by the shouting and the running, swelling the numbers to about fifty.

What happened next could have been almost comical had the individuals involved not been so sickening. The police stopped running, having realised the incident had been dealt with, and began to disperse. The mob stopped at a junction, not sure what to do. They cast their eyes around them, trying to work out what to do next. Some of them clearly felt inspired to demonstrate 'leadership qualities', by shouting 'Come on, England', 'Let's get at them, England', or 'Stick together'.

The essence of their problem was they wanted a fight, but there was no one around who wanted to fight them. They were all psyched up, some of them clearly coked up, itching for a violent confrontation, and for all their rampaging round the back streets of a foreign capital, they couldn't find one.

'The Dutch, where are the fucking Dutch?'

'The Dutch aren't interested!'

'So who the fuck are we going to fight then?'

'What about the Turks?'

'We've arranged to meet the Turks at Dam Square at one o'clock.'

Given that this exchange took place at after half-past midnight, I thought they'd better get going if they didn't want to be late. Looking back, I think this might actually have been empty bravado.

'So who are we going to fight now then?'

'Wogs! Just get wogs! Get any wogs you can find.'

This was the cue for a small series of sickening attacks on any black person who happened to be passing. Two or three totally innocent blokes were given a kicking by these English anti-heroes. Separately, of course. In each case by five or six onto one. Cowardly attacks by arseholes who'd come abroad to fight for their country, as they sadly imagined it.

One of them in particular caught my eye. Not because he was a particularly striking piece of humanity. On the contrary, he caught my attention because he looked a complete drip. Not short, but skinny, bespectacled, wearing a white shirt and a dark baseball cap. Shouting vile racist abuse and incitements to violence, I remembered him most precisely because he looked like the sort of person who would be bullied at school. Now he was part of a gang, where he could play the hero. Victim turned bully, I should imagine. I knew the type. The sort whose idea of a good scrap was running in from the fringes, hitting someone anonymously from behind and then running away again. My contempt for him was total.

I might have forgotten him by now, were it not for the fact that the same bloke was singled out by the *Panorama* programme, after they'd filmed him with a hidden camera. They identified him as Justin Barrall from Leicester. According to the programme, he had been convicted for threatening behaviour at football matches. It seemed he couldn't always run away fast enough.

I would probably have forgotten him even so, were it not for a strange twist of fate. He contacted the FSA.

Apparently he was not happy that *Panorama* had identified him wrongly. The caller said it was definitely him on the film, rampaging around the narrow streets of Amsterdam's red-light district with a mob of nasty racist thugs committing acts of vicious random violence, but they'd given out the wrong name. He wanted to put the record straight. His real name was not Justin Barrall.

He went on to tell us his real name, and asked us to help him put the record straight. I couldn't help thinking he'd missed the point.

Eindhoven

Monday 12th June

KEVIN WAS READY for the big kick-off. A lot of preparation had gone into this game, now was the moment of truth. Eindhoven, Monday 12th June, 2000.

It had been suggested, not without some justification, that maybe Kevin's strengths lay more on the PR side of things. Not only here at Euro 2000 but also back at Newcastle, he'd struck up a good rapport with the media, affable, always willing to oblige. But as a coach? Did he have the tactical shrewdness to succeed at this level? There was clearly going to be more required here than just making the players like him, jollying them along. It was more than just motivation that was needed now — what about a system? Would every English player running onto the field that day know exactly what was required of him? And formation — one upfront and pack the midfield? 4–4–2 or 3–5–2? Wing backs for width? Decisions had to be made.

First thing to do was to count the players and make sure he could field a full side.

Maybe this would be a good point to clarify, just in case any misunderstandings have crept in, that we're not talking — yet — about the Euro 2000 group game between England and Portugal. I think it would be safe to assume that for that game, the coach would know fairly well in advance how many players he would have at his disposal, even if there were still selection issues to resolve.

Worrying about whether or not we'd be able to turn out a full eleven was however a real factor in my pre-match preparations for my international debut as a coach. The game in question was a fans' friendly match between an England side pulled together – dragged kicking and screaming in some cases – by the FSA, and Holland, in the form of a side assembled by the PSV Eindhoven fan project. It promised to be a good laugh, but its primary purpose was as a media event, to highlight a more positive, and I'd argue a more typical side of English football fans to audiences both at home and in Holland. It was also to draw attention to one particular initiative by the Fans' Embassy which had gone down really well with our hosts, an effort to raise funds for the victims of the horrendous tragedy in nearby Enschede. An explosion in a fireworks warehouse had devastated the town, killing twenty people, injuring scores of others and leaving hundreds of families homeless.

The game itself was preceded by an almost slick press conference attended by Dutch and English television crews. Jardine PR had thoughtfully arranged for a very professional-looking backdrop to be on hand, we had arranged for the English media to be informed and Dutch reporters had been summoned by the very talented Marloes Frijhoff. Marloes was on secondment from her job as commercial manager for the Go Ahead Eagles football club for the duration of the tournament to work as press officer for Eurosupport, the organisation co-ordinating the international fans' embassies in the host cities and the teams of 'fan coaches' from each country. Taking part in the press conference were a representative of the fan project in Enschede, which was to receive the money raised among England fans, and a celebrity special guest.

The presence of a star in our midst not only enhanced the status of our press conference in the eyes of the media people present, it also very conclusively found us a winner for one of the competitions we'd launched in the fanzine. The item in question was 'The van de Kerkhof Challenge'.

Rene and Willy van de Kerkhof are two of Eindhoven's most famous sons, and certainly its most celebrated twin sons. Both had highly successful football careers. They played together for Twente Enschede before both joining, at same time – must be a twin thing – PSV in time to win the Dutch league in 1975, and again in 1976. The most high-profile game they played together in was the 1978 World Cup Final in Buenos Aires.

Rene van de Kerkhof was at the centre of controversy before a ball was kicked, when the Argentinian captain Daniel Passarella objected to the plaster cast Rene was wearing on his right wrist. Gamesmanship, it would seem; to have the maximum unsettling effect on the Dutch, the hosts waited until after the national anthems and other formalities were out of the way before saying anything. This even though Rene had worn the cast in every game since he had injured it in his side's opening game against Iran. Kick-off was delayed by nine minutes, disconcerting for the Dutch but probably causing paroxysms among all the television producers from every country with expensive satellite time booked. Ah well, so at least some good came out of it. Every cloud has a silver lining.

So the van de Kerkhof twins seemed an obvious choice for inclusion in our fanzine. We warmed up with a 'Willy or Rene' quiz:

Was it a Willy or a Rene who:

1 Delayed the start of the '78 World Cup Final because of the plaster cast on his arm?

2 Starred in the Hollywood film about the release of a giant whale back into the ocean?

3 Had a No. 1 hit single, 'Save Your Love', with Renato in 1982?

4 Saw his name used as an affectionate nickname for their penis by millions of small British boys?

5 Invented a best-selling and fast-acting remedy for indigestion?

6 As a young lion, was the mascot for the 1966 World Cup in England?

7 Played the heroic bartender in the dark and ironic comedy 'Allo, Allo'?

8 Was characterised as 'wicked' in a series of cutting cartoon books?

9 Recorded a number of albums with John Otway during his 'wild' phase?

Anyone who still felt up to it after that taxing interrogation was then invited to take the 'van de Kerkhof Challenge'. We offered a prize to the first England fan to find local resident Willy van de Kerkhof in Eindhoven and bring his autograph to our embassy van.

As it turned out, we didn't have to settle merely for Willy's autograph. We got his brother instead. Rene arrived at our press conference keen to offer his support for what we'd been doing. He spoke warmly about the England fans, and was then pressed into service to kick off the game. I felt quite honoured to be photographed shaking hands with a man who had played in two World Cup Finals (Rene had also come on as a substitute in the 1974 Final in Germany), but sadly we were unable to award the challenge prize to Rene as he did not bring us Willy's autograph. Apparently the two brothers aren't speaking, having fallen out over their commercial work at the last World Cup. A bit harsh of us maybe, but rules are rules.

As for the game, the history books will show that England won 7–5, and I'd like to report that it was inspired tactical decisions by the coach combined with superior fitness and ball skills that won the day. I'd like to, but honesty prevents me. The result has much more to do with Dutch generosity, which is meant not as a euphemism for them having given the ball away cheaply in midfield but as a reference to their giving us their goalkeeper for the second half and playing without one themselves.

In an illustration of how misleading television pictures can be, the Dutch news footage showed a clip of one England goal which looked very classy, coolly finished by Glen Gibson from an inch-perfect through ball by Paul Thomas, which left the goalkeeper apparently nowhere. The keeper was of course at the other end of the pitch at the time, keeping goal for us; the fact that on the basis of his one half for us he was our man of the match might help to keep our achievement in proportion. It was end-to-end stuff – they were always up our end, and we wondered when it would.

To be fair, we'd assembled a team at short notice from meagre resources – I wasn't kidding about counting players – and though we'd been kindly supplied with shorts and socks, footwear was another issue, and at least one of our number took to the pitch in brogues.

The game was played at the stadium of the other professional team in Eindhoven, EVV, who play in the second division, and the core of the opposition consisted of the EVV youth team. Which of course meant that they were all young, competent and very fit, in sharp contrast to our side, which contained TV cameramen who'd made the mistake of standing still for too long and being pressed into service. Still, in terms of what it was intended to do, the game was a triumph, which is sadly more than could be said for England's other match that day.

Eindhoven that Monday was great. The town really started filling up from about midday, as train after train disgorged its noisy contents, who were then drawn to the Market Square, less than five minutes walk away. The central square in any town when there's an international football match being played has this magnetic quality, especially if as is so often the case they are surrounded by bars. For the purposes required, Eindhoven's market fitted the bill admirably. One long side of the square in particular consisted almost exclusively of bars and restaurants. One of these was the Cafe Centraal, appropriately enough in the middle of this long side, and the enterprising owner in collaboration with the local police had installed on his first floor balcony a massive sound system, from which music was played throughout most of the day. The opposite side of the square (the oblong, I suppose) was mainly made up of shops which were closed for the day. Many had grilles over the windows, which was very handy for the essential purpose of hanging flags and banners. As a result large expanses of buildings were hidden by St. George's flags adorned with some clue as to their origin, whether that be the name of a football club, a town or village, a part of a town, a team and a town, or even in one or two cases just the name of a pub.

As I've said, most of the shops and businesses – apart of course from the ones for whom the arrival of the England roadshow meant their best takings for years — were closed. This was not, however, as some reporters tried to suggest, out of fear for the safety of people and property while the marauding hordes of English were in town. It was much more to do with the fact that it was a public holiday throughout Holland, something that had been printed in Dutch diaries a long time before the Euro 2000 fixtures were finalised.

The weather was beautiful, hot and sunny, and the atmosphere in the Market Square was relaxed and pleasant. Everybody was involved in that strange ritual played out at all tournaments, where they assemble in one central place, in numbers far too great to fit into the bars, then stand around all day looking at everybody else doing exactly the same. Occasionally you'd have a bit of a wander, see who you could meet, strike up conversations with people you didn't yet know, and in this way new friendships are formed that will last in some cases for years, possibly even long enough to see England win something.

Usually in these circumstances an impromptu game of football will break out, and this was no exception, at one stage a highly informal game involving England fans and the local police. Before long the square was too full to allow the ball to be kicked more than two yards in any horizontal direction, let alone for a really flowing, passing game to flourish.

Clearly in these circumstances there would have to be modifications to the rules of the football game being played, and sure enough it moved onto another plane. Literally, in that the only way for the ball to be kicked was up. So wherever it landed, someone would pick it up and drop-kick it into the air again, and it would land in all probability on someone's head at the other side of the square. That individual would then be the object of ridicule by his mates, while one of them launched the ball heavenwards again. Some particularly mischievous little scamps started aiming deliberately for the balconies on the first and second floors on the 'pubs' side of the square – there was little danger, as the heat meant that most of the windows were open anyway, and the balconies were mostly occupied too, by people trying to catch the ball. On the rare occasions that they did, they were momentarily bemused as to what to do with it; it took a few seconds before they realised that all they really could do was throw it back down so the game could continue.

Of course every time the ball went up it also had to come down. Inevitably the time came when the ball landed somewhere it was probably better if it hadn't. A waitress emerged from a bar holding a tray with a dozen freshly poured beers when there was a sudden impact from above, sending the beers flying and soaking her. There was a sharp intake of breath from the fans in the square, or at least from those who had had an unobstructed view of what had happened, and a huge collective sigh of relief when it became clear she had seen the funny side and was very amused as she went back for a new tray, to a round of applause. No doubt those in the local council who'd pushed for an insistence on plastic containers felt entirely vindicated. A few minutes later, a small group of laughing and smiling policemen in shirtsleeves 'confiscated' the ball, to a light-hearted token round of booing.

There is clearly a thriving surrealist wing among England fans. At one stage during the day, I saw another version of the game being played in the square, except instead of a ball, a large wet fish was being used. It was thrown, rather than kicked, of course. You'd have to be daft to start kicking a fish up in the air. And they don't bounce, I noticed.

At one point in the afternoon, I found myself on a second floor balcony overlooking the square, the vantage point of the

BBC Radio Five Live 'studio' for the day. As I watched the ball game in progress, and saw the thousands of England fans milling about in anticipation of the match to come, basking in the sunshine; as I watched the white skin reddening before my eyes; as I listened to the laughter and the singing; as I counted the varieties of ridiculous shorts and even more bizarre headgear, I thought to myself: only someone who has never been and done this, who has never experienced it, could fail to understand why people travel without tickets. They do it because there's always an off-chance, a hope that they might get into the ground, but even if they don't, they can be part of this. They can say they were there, they joined the party. This was a great day out, even before the game kicked off. Watching the match in a bar after a day like this does not mean you've had a wasted trip. You've been part of a big occasion.

Only someone who'd never been part of an experience could ever have dreamt up the campaign that the British Government launched prior to the World Cup in 1998. Over a million pounds they spent on television advertising as part of their 'no ticket, no travel' strategy.

Remember the adverts? Not strictly speaking adverts, I suppose, more 'government information films', in the fine tradition of the ones about unplugging all electrical appliances before you go to bed, and not letting Grandad fall asleep in his armchair while he's smoking. These ones were about the England fan – who I always though looked vaguely like Frank Skinner – turning up at the turnstile at some French stadium, only to be turned away heart-broken because his name didn't match that on the ticket. A poignant tale, and all designed to convince us that even if you did get a ticket, you wouldn't get in, so you may as well stay at home. Talk about missing the point.

Over £1 million they spent on that advert – what a waste of money! The most unrealistic piece of television since the Clangers fought the Daleks for the WWF tag team championship belt – and won.

I've been on holidays that were a lot less fun than that day in Eindhoven, and I didn't get into the game that night. I was a ticketless fan, a term that's still used in the media as if it has negative connotations. As if to imply 'Well, they haven't got tickets, so they're obviously not going for the game – they must be up to no good. Stop them travelling, seize their passports!'

There are glaring flaws in this argument, of course. Not least that it's impossible to tell the difference between a 'ticketless fan' and a 'holidaymaker who likes football'. If I go to Rome on holiday in September, am I a ticketless fan of the next Lazio game? For all I've said about the delights of Eindhoven, you'd have a scrap on your hands from the Brabant tourist board if you said it was out of the question that anyone would ever want to go there on holiday.

No, anybody who's ever been to an international tournament knows that there are always people who travel without tickets, who go just for the crack, and it doesn't mean that there's a problem. Even the organisers themselves know that's the case; if not, big screens would never have been invented.

The other side of this is of course that a lot of people who travel without tickets do succeed in picking them up on the 'black market'; it always happens at international tournaments. If there aren't many about, then the price goes up, but you can always find a way to get one if you're prepared to pay.

A lot of fans have mixed feelings about black market tickets. Nobody likes being ripped off, and no one likes to see some of the unsavoury characters who make a very good living out of touting lining their pockets at the expense of genuine fans. But for a lot of fans, the only way they ever get a ticket is through unofficial channels, because the official ones don't look after ordinary supporters. Only when we get a system that puts all the tickets into the hands of genuine supporters at realistic prices will we see an end to touting, because only when every ticket goes to someone who desperately wants to see the game will there not be any up for sale.

It really annoys me the way the football authorities deal with this issue. They introduce enormously elaborate and expensive systems for logging the names and addresses of everyone who is supplied with a ticket, all in the name of segregation and security. That's a red herring, by the way; look at all the games England have played at major tournaments recently, and you can instantly see that segregation has completely broken down, there are English everywhere. Yet there have been precious few problems inside the stadia.

But all the measures proposed by the football authorities to shore up the gaps in their system are punitive ones aimed at the fans themselves. It's the ordinary supporter who is faced with the possibility of paying over the odds for a ticket, and it's the ordinary supporter who is faced with the prospect of being denied admission, or even being arrested, if they are checked up on at the turnstile.

Yet the ticketing systems adopted by FIFA and UEFA guarantee the existence of a black market. UEFA's system this time round was by no means the worst. They had at least scrapped the ridiculous category of tickets from the last World Cup of 'Approved Tour Operators'. This was an openly corrupt system of licensed touting. Companies were invited to submit sealed bids (bribes, in effect) to FIFA to buy a licence to become an Approved Tour Operator, or ATO.

Not surprisingly, FIFA has yet to reveal how much the

organising committee made out of this tendering system. We can hazard a guess though. There were 17 companies accorded ATO status in total. One of them has let slip that their successful bid comprised a lump sum of £500,000, and a premium of £5 on top of the face value of every ticket they received. Now I don't know if these figures represent the highest or lowest successful bid, so let's for the sake of argument say it's an average. If that were so, then the tournament organisers will have received £8,500,000 in lump sums. And having supplied to ATOs 8% of all the World Cup match tickets, a total of 200,000 tickets, then they're looking at another £1 million on top. So for the granting of licences to tout tickets, in effect, they may have generated an extra nine-and-a-half million pounds. But don't worry, we know FIFA's motto — it's 'for the good of the game'.

ATOs then in effect bought the right to sell on the tickets as part of a hospitality package, and they determined the prices. The prices they charged were naturally often far in excess of what anybody could seriously argue was the value of the other elements of the package. They were exploiting the fact that many fans were so desperate to see the games that if that was the only way to get hold of a ticket, then that's what they'd have to buy. It's been for years a form of glorified touting. And the provision of a glass of warm, flat once-sparkling wine in the committee room of a run-down workingmen's club just half-a-mile from the stadium legally allows a price mark up of several hundred per cent on the grounds that the ticket has now become part of a champagne reception.

(I should perhaps point out that not all hospitality packages were downmarket affairs purely designed as a cover for a price hike. Some were extremely high quality events held in exclusive surroundings, with cordon bleu cuisine, the finest wines and celebrity hosts. These events are popular forms of corporate entertainment, and very much appreciated by those who are invited to them. But do we really want people like that infesting perfectly respectable football grounds?)

Credit where it's due, at least for Euro 2000 UEFA scrapped the category of licensed touts. But they did still adopt a system where one in three tickets were kept out of the reach of ordinary fans. They also persisted with one aspect of tournament ticketing which infuriates me, and which guarantees the creation of a black market. They put the tickets on sale before the qualification process was complete.

Selling all the tickets for a tournament as far in advance as possible is an obvious, logical thing to do – if you're the organisers' accountant. Get the money in well in advance – a year in advance if possible. No reason why it should be sitting around in the pockets or bank accounts of all those football customers – sorry, fans – when it could be working for us. Think of the interest!

And of course, a year in advance we have all the information needed to put the tickets on sale, haven't we? We know which town and stadium they'll be held in, and what date and time, don't we? Then let's get selling.

Perfectly logical. But from the point of view of a fan who wants to go and see his or her team, there's a slight drawback. You don't know which of these games your team's going to be playing in. It's a big guessing game – so you have a stab, and order tickets for matches 4, 11 and 16 in the hope that you hit lucky.

Even then, some country's fans were luckier than others. The Czech Republic won every one of their twelve qualifiers, so they were fairly sure they'd be at Euro 2000 quite early on. But by the time the tickets went on sale – in May 1999 –

England and Scotland fans didn't know if they'd even qualify. It would be six months before they could be sure their team would be in the tournament.

Eventually the draw is made, and England are going to play Germany. That's the one you want! And you check your receipt and find that unfortunately you haven't got England v Germany, but you've just paid seventy quid for a good seat at . . . Yugoslavia v Slovenia.

And back at UEFA headquarters, or the Euro 2000 foundation, or wherever the accountants are based, someone is pointing out another advantage of their system. They've sold out every game! That would never have happened if people had *known* they were buying tickets at seventy quid each for Yugoslavia v Slovenia!

It's outrageous. No other entertainment industry – and that's what they keep telling us football is these days – would dare to try it. Can you imagine a music promoter organising a series of concerts, but not telling you who's playing where and when? You decide to treat your old Irish granny to front row seats at the Daniel O'Donnell concert for her birthday, but when the big day comes, she finds she's in the prime dandruff-and-deafness zone at the Metallica gig.

Or you pluck up the courage to ask out someone you've fancied for ages with the words "I've got a couple of cinema tickets", and you end up impressing them with . . . the Pokemon movie.

They wouldn't get away with it – so why should the football authorities get away with doing it to us?

To compound all these problems, this system creates exactly the situation the organisers say they're determined to stamp out – the black market. It stands to reason, to me at least, that if you contrive to sell people loads of tickets for games they don't particularly want to see, and sell the tickets for the games they are desperate to see to another set of people who don't really want them, then those tickets are going to change hands, one way or another. The least the organisers could do in the circumstances would be to organise some form of official exchange network, where they can monitor the swaps, check there are no price mark-ups taking place, that sort of thing. Oh no, that's too expensive, or inconvenient or something.

Of course the exchange networks develop. And if they're persecuted off the street corners, they'll pop up elsewhere, like on the Internet.

The only answer the authorities have is repression of the fans. They'll step up police powers to arrest people trading in tickets. They'll build in elaborate computer references so that they can – theoretically, if not in practice – check the identity of every ticket holder, and prevent them seeing the game they've paid for. They'll do anything to stamp out the black market, except the one thing that would make a difference – put the tickets directly into the hands of the people who most want to see the games.

That might take a revolution in ticketing methods, a whole different set of priorities, so maybe it's asking a lot. But holding on for six months before putting tickets on sale – still six months before kick-off – so that people know what they're buying? Surely that's not too much to ask?

Back in Eindhoven, we were taking loads of calls on our FSA hotline from people who had ordered tickets quite legitimately from Euro 2000, paid for them, but who then hadn't been in when the postman called to deliver them. The precious tickets were of course sent recorded delivery, so when there was no one in to sign for them (maybe they'd rashly gone to work or something), they were returned to sender – in Rotterdam.

Apparently the small print authorised the Euro 2000 foundation in these circumstances to resell the tickets without even refunding the purchase price. But of course a lot of fans had booked and paid for travel and accommodation on the strength of the tickets, and actually wanted to go to the games. Believe it or not, it took some pressure and representation to convince Euro 2000 not to resell the tickets. Instead, they said, they would hold on to them, and the buyers could pick them up – in Rotterdam.

Now, very few people had planned to travel to Eindhoven via Rotterdam. It was going to be very inconvenient. And if you'd arranged a flying visit to Charleroi for the Germany or Romania games, it would be bloody impossible. Eventually the FSA Embassy team managed to secure the concession that if fans turned up at the stadium accompanied by one of our embassy staff, and with all the relevant documentation, they would be allowed to take their seat without having to go to Rotterdam.

All's well that ends well, you could say, but it was just one more indication that the ticketing system revealed an organising authority with no respect for the most important people in football – the fans.

The fabulous pre-match atmosphere continued all day in Eindhoven, and eventually the time came for the lucky ones with tickets to make the short walk to the stadium. The biggest controversy anyone in the media had managed to find – and these people do try very hard to find a controversy – was the policy of serving low-alcohol beer to the fans in the square. I must have fielded a dozen phone calls on the subject, including funnily enough at least three from Scottish papers. Their angle seemed to be to try to get me to say that English fans had been singled out for crap beer, that there was an insult intended that we couldn't be trusted, and that we were being ripped off. I couldn't help thinking that these same reporters, while trying to generate some excitement about the alcohol issue, would have been just as hysterical, if not more so, had they been able to report that the naive Dutch had been serving full-strength lager to England fans all day.

As it was, they all seemed disappointed when I told them that the police had told us months earlier that this would be their policy. Their theory about the English being singled out to be insulted or ripped off collapsed too when it was pointed out that the beer in question is well known as 'event beer'. It is always served to the locals and everybody else, whenever there is some sort of street carnival taking place.

It did occur to me that thanks to all the publicity, every England fan drinking in Eindhoven that day would be under the impression that they were drinking lager that was 2.5% proof, and may well adjust the pace or quantity of their consumption accordingly. I knew however that it was not the case that every bar was serving only event beer; it was a recommendation rather than an instruction from the police, and some bar owners had opted to serve the same beer as usual.

I wonder what the implications would be for anyone arrested for drunkenness that evening. Would the same Scottish tabloids who'd been trying to find a story about the insult of the weak lager then leap to the defence of the poor innocent soul who'd been unwittingly sold full-strength beer and had drunk more than usual as a consequence? I have my doubts.

Most bar owners did go along with the 'event beer' recommendation however, and were disappointed that they were nonetheless instructed by the police to close early after the match (I think it may have been another 'recommendation', but with a hint of 'if you know what's good for you . . .'). The bars had their own reasons for wanting to prolong the party, of course. One bar owner told me that the previous evening (Sunday) he'd taken over fifteen thousand guilders compared to a usual Sunday night trade of four to five thousand – and this was before most of the English support hit town.

One other part of the success of the Eindhoven experience worthy of comment – especially now that hindsight has allowed a comparison with Belgium to be made – was the policing. Like a good referee, you hardly noticed them at the time; they didn't seem a major factor in the situation. The fact that the day passed off so well I think has to be down at least in part to the way the police and the authorities in Eindhoven handled it. The policing was high-profile but low friction. There were plenty of police about, but mainly in shirtsleeves and smiling faces. They were easy-going, patient, indulgent of high spirits but politely firm when it came to needing to nip in the bud any potential problems.

They were quite happy to chat with England fans – the remarkable Dutch facility with the English language was a major factor here – and didn't seem to regard every Englishman as a potential hooligan. Every now and again, a couple of mounted police would walk their horses through the square, as a subtle reminder that they did have other options available to them. Later in the evening, small patrols would tour the town, but far from cruising the streets in riot vans, they would walk through the crowds and maybe ten yards behind them a group of four or six in more paramilitary style gear but still as relaxed, then some further twenty yards behind a couple on horseback.

There were a few occasions where a couple of police would approach a group of English fans who were just starting to get a bit too rowdy, or even just a bit too numerous for where they were gathered, and with a laugh disperse them, in such a way that for anyone to take offence would have brought immediate reproach from their own mates. The police were so reasonable.

On occasions I was reminded of the Dutch police in the Harry Enfield sketch, where the two policemen, having introduced themselves as gay lovers, share a joint as they sit in their car watching the world go by. But nobody should be under any illusion that the Eindhoven police were a soft touch. This was all a carefully planned strategy, and I didn't doubt for a minute that if there had been any major problems, they would not have hesitated using whatever force they deemed necessary to sort it out.

If anything, within Holland the Eindhoven police have a reputation for being strict and less tolerant than elsewhere. Eindhoven police record over 20% of all football-related arrests in Holland. In the meetings we had with police officials before the tournament however, the Eindhoven police leaders, like Bert van het Schip, made clear that their emphasis would be on welcoming English fans to their city, in the expectation that they would respond accordingly. Bert told us 'Police intervention with planes and tanks is not a good approach', which we found immensely reassuring.

I believe that the tone of the reception England received in Eindhoven, which was universally welcoming and positive, made a real difference in how the bulk of the England fans responded. I lost count early in the day of the number of English supporters who commented to me about how friendly and helpful local people were, and how good the atmosphere was. I cannot accept the argument put forward by some commentators after Charleroi that the reason that there had not been similar problems in Eindhoven was because the 'hooligans' had not gone there. There may well have been more of the unpleasant characters in Belgium, both in absolute numbers and as a proportion of the total number of English fans. But I had seen some of these characters at their worst in Amsterdam, and I'd recognised a fair few of them again in Eindhoven. They were there, but the generally positive atmosphere left them isolated. There were attempts to start choruses of 'No Surrender' in the Market Square, but they got so little echo that they tailed away. These characters feed off hostility and tension, and there was precious little of either in Eindhoven.

At about five past nine local time that evening, you could have been forgiven for thinking that there was about to be a perfect end to a perfect day. All the talk about how this team really could go all the way didn't seem quite so absurd after Paul Scholes had scored in the third minute, and Steve McManaman followed up minutes after with a second. Back in the Fans' Embassy building where I was watching the game, even the neutrals were impressed, and started to discuss the prospects of an England-Holland final. Perhaps now they remember me as the wise Englishman who judges football so well because I seemed slightly dubious at the time. It was simply because I had enjoyed enough of Kevin Keegan's teams to know that a two-nil lead is no guarantee of victory . . .

Eindhoven

Tuesday 13th – Thursday 15th June

NORMALLY BETWEEN YOUR team's games at an international tournament, you enjoy a couple of days' relaxation. When you're part of a Fans' Embassy though, you do things a bit differently.

No sitting around soaking up the sun outside a welcoming bar. For us, the day after a game was one of the busiest. Two days later we wanted to be in Charleroi, ready to distribute the latest edition of our fanzine. Which meant that tomorrow, it had to be printed. Which meant that it had to be written, edited and proofread today.

So most of us settled down for a long day in the Fans' Embassy building slaving over a hot computer. Most, but not all. As a result of the lottery that was the ticketing system, some of the team had ended up with tickets for other exotic games, and were generously given time off to travel to see them. Adam went off to Rotterdam to see Norway's surprise victory over Spain.

As for Jim – well, we'd all had good laugh at Jim's expense. Jim it was who, by the luck of the draw, had paid seventy quid for a ticket for a game in Charleroi. Unluckily for him, it had been for the only game in Charleroi not involving England. Jim was off to see the unfancied Yugoslavia against the even less fancied Slovenia. Ah well, never mind, at least while he was there he could check out the latest info about the town.

Jim had the last laugh, of course, as the game no-one wanted to see turned into the game of the tournament so far. Even the Slovenian team looked as though they couldn't believe it when within an hour they found themselves three up. To those of us not really watching the match, it just confirmed for us how low the Yugoslavian team must have sunk, and we chuckled again to ourselves at Jim's bad luck, in a caring sort of way.

Three goals in seven minutes and it was all-square. Unbelievable. Two scored by former Villa, er, striker, Savo Milosevic. Even more unbelievable. Jim came back convinced he'd got his money's worth from a fascinating game. Yugoslavia would never be involved in a game with a turn-around like that again. Well, not for a week or so, anyway.

Turning out sixteen pages of fanzine in less than twenty-four hours was not going to be easy. So we'd cheated, by preparing some of it in advance. One of the parts of the first edition which had gone down best was the back cover, where we'd reproduced some of the more memorable things that Kevin Keegan had come out with in his time as a media pundit.

Wise Words from Our Great Leader

13 sayings of Kevin Keegan

1 'England can end the millennium as it started – as the greatest football nation in the world.'

2 'In some ways, cramp is worse than having a broken leg.'

3 'Goalkeepers aren't born today until they're in their late twenties or thirties.'

4 'The tide is very much in our court.'

5 'They're the second best team in the world, and there's no higher praise that that.'

6 'England have the best fans in the world, and Scotland's fans are second to none.'

7 'I don't think there's anyone bigger or smaller than Maradona.'

8 'You can't do better than go away from home and get a draw.'

9 'They compare Steve McManaman to Steve Heighway and he's nothing like him, but I can see why – it's because he's a bit different.'

10 'I came to Nantes two years ago and it's much the same today, except that it's totally different.'

11 'I know what is around the corner – I just don't know where the corner is. But the onus is on us to perform and we must control the bandwagon.'

12 'The 33 or 34-year-olds will be 36 or 37 by the time the next World Cup comes around, if they're not careful.'

13 'It's understandable that people are keeping on eye on the pot and another up the chimney.'

We had plenty more where they had come from, already prepared. Brian McNally was lined up to do five pages for us: three pages on our next opponents, of which two would be pen portraits of the players in their squad, and another two pages of his own thoughts on results and prospects. Brian's copy was always fresh and despite more than our share of technical problems, he always delivered it in good time. Honestly, you'd think he was a professional.

So that was six pages accounted for. Our embassy sponsors, the mobile phone company One 2 One, were given two pages in each edition. Jardine PR had thoughtfully arranged for these pages to be prepared in advance, and the printer already had them, so that was two more sorted.

We had a bit of a plan for the format of the rest. The centre-page spread would be on the host city, giving useful and up-to-date information. Page 10 would be our anti-racist page. That left us five pages, including the front cover, to report on what had been going on off the pitch, to offer our wise comments, and to try to be amusing and entertaining.

It's testimony to the quality and the hard work of the team that we always ended up leaving stuff out – there was no shortage of material. The biggest discussion usually revolved around the front page. This had to be eye-catching and if at all possible, topical. For ease of design, we'd decided in advance to do it 'Private Eye-style', that is a big photo with a speech bubble or a caption. What was the talking point we had to address?

The biggest item of controversy in the press after the Portugal game had been David Beckham's middle-finger salute to a section of fans who had been giving him a bit of abuse. I hadn't been at the game, the incident wasn't highlighted on Dutch TV, so I didn't feel qualified to comment on it. If anything my instinctive reaction was to defend fans' rights to criticise, and anyway, the FSA Embassy had a general policy of not getting involved in issues around individual players. We tried as far as possible to stick to issues which united

England fans, our opinions on players were nobody's but our own and worth no more than anybody else's either, plus we knew that fans' opinions on Beckham were divided anyway.

When I did find out what had been shouted at Beckham, I was disgusted. Anyone who can shout at an England player or anyone else that they hope his child gets cancer is sick themselves. That sort of insult is indefensible.

There is an interesting debate to be had about the abuse of footballers, about what's acceptable, what's not, and how and where to draw the line. Some forms of abuse are clearly absolutely unacceptable in any circumstances, such as racism. For me this is non-negotiable. Racism is a vile prejudice, and no amount of protestation that 'abuse is all part of the game' can ever disguise the fact that racism underlies systematic oppression and discrimination, at times to the point of murderous hatred, within society. That can never be a laughing matter. Some people in football have tried to draw a parallel between abuse on racial grounds and having a go at someone who has a dodgy haircut. Shaka Hislop, currently West Ham's goalkeeper and a leading campaigner against racism, answered that argument perfectly for me when he said,

> Simply to class people who have gone through so much hardship historically, such oppression historically, people who even today can't get jobs because of their colour, can't get jobs because of the accent they speak with; to put them in the same melting pot as someone who went to the wrong barber is atrocious.

It would be hard to argue too that general standards of taste and decency should not apply in football. Normal rules about what you say in front of kids hold just as much in football grounds as elsewhere, though I couldn't personally promise not to swear at a match (and I'd defy anyone to watch some of the games I've endured without cursing). I would however make a distinction between foul, crude and obscene abuse aimed at an individual, and giving undirected expression to frustration at a missed chance, say.

Having piously stated the obvious however, I must admit that I do get irritated by those people – and campaigns – that seek to make everybody be nice to each other. There's a serious point here – by lumping racism in with swearing, for example, I think you run the risk of trivialising an important message, and diminishing the impact of anti-racist campaigns.

There's also the point though that without the banter, the wit, the odd swear word, yes to an extent even the abuse, well it just wouldn't be football, would it?

Maybe this is a reaction to attempts to sanitise the game by those wanting it to be even more commercially saleable. Even from their point of view I think they've got it wrong. Most of my best experiences of football have involved laughing at it, and more often than not swearing at it. Abusing a player can be a really good laugh too.

So where's this line to be drawn, then? I don't think there are many people about who are so po-faced that they'd object to shouting 'dodgy keeper' at an error-prone goalie, or David James as he is better known. That itself deals with the argument that players are 'just doing their job', and that 'you wouldn't expect anyone else to have to put up with abuse at their workplace'. This is not a normal workplace, part of the wages players receive takes into account the fact that they do their work in a public place, before a crowd, and under critical scrutiny, shall we say.

Interesting idea though, spreading the habit to other jobs. It might be an effective form of motivation for those employed in public transport if queues who've waited longer than they should burst into a chorus of 'dodgy driver' when the bus eventually arrives. Or if when we get someone else's mail delivered in error, we open the front door and shout after the postman 'You're shit, and you know you are!' Ask the next meter reader to prove his identity by bellowing 'Who are ya? Who are ya?' through the letterbox. Though it's probably advisable not to proposition your partner by shouting 'You're going down with the Mackems'.

Another argument I've heard is that you shouldn't give somebody stick for something they can't do anything to change. Proponents of this point of view often use terms like 'ageism', 'heightism', even 'gingerism'. The problem here is defining exactly what people can help and what they can't, such have been the advances in modern science. OK, there's still not been much impact made on stopping the ageing process, and football in platform boots may not be particularly graceful. But hair colour? That can certainly be changed, and there are plenty of examples of where it has been done to great comic effect. Who can forget the Neil Lennon's hilarious bleached blonde look last season?

And to all those who say fans shouldn't have a go at someone for baldness, I say this: what then is the point of Mark Draper?

Some of the most entertaining moments of football matches come when players are baited, providing there's an element of wit and originality present. Best of all is when they've clearly brought it on themselves, by some act of stupidity or perhaps a parting shot on leaving for another club. As long as there is no risk to life and limb, I'm all in favour too of the imaginative use of visual aids. For instance, when Chris Waddle left Newcastle for Spurs, he was quoted as praising the difference between the two clubs in the choice of post-match meal. Apparently at Spurs the team would all go to a restaurant, whereas Newcastle's team coach would stop at a chip shop. (I've witnessed this, by the way, and there can be no greater recommendation for the Wetherby Whaler.) To my mind, he entirely deserved the barrage of chip wrappers and cold batter he got on his return to St. James's Park. I'm even prepared to suspend any doubts I would normally have about people who waste Mars bars when the target of their volley of confectionery is the returning Paul Gascoigne.

Being abused positively feeds the desire of some players, inspiring them to greater things, which is always a danger. I used to love opposing fans booing David Ginola when he played for Newcastle; I hold my head in my hands nervously when the same thing happens at St. James's nowadays. And responding in good spirit to being sledged can endear the unlikeliest players in the hearts of opposing fans. I remember Vinnie Jones, for one, being applauded off the field after clearly entering into the spirit of what was being said to him. Admittedly he had played a blinder too, his performance as stand-in goalkeeper keeping the margin of his Wimbledon side's defeat down to 6–1.

As I said, there's an interesting debate to be had, and that is by no means the end of it. It's ironic though that this debate has been occasioned by clearly unacceptable abuse dished out to someone who usually deserves all he gets, on one of the rare occasions when he didn't. The match against Portugal had been one of the few games where Beckham hadn't let the side down, he was one of the team's better players on the night, and he did make both the goals. So for what it's worth, in my opinion he didn't deserve that sick abuse.

Beckham's profile generates a lot of the attention he gets, and he goes out his way – very profitably – to court publicity, so he has to take the rough with the smooth. I didn't really have a problem with the stick that Beckham got after his sending-off against Argentina in the last World Cup, though death threats were a bit much, because in that case he brought it on himself by his own petulant action, and he did damage the team.

But all this philosophical discussion still left us with a front cover to devise, and Beckham's retaliatory single finger salute was still the news headline. So we settled after some debate on a Beckham front cover, with Glenn Hoddle counting out instructions on his fingers to Beckham, and saying 'David, when you're counting to ten, start with your thumb, not your middle finger.' Clever, eh? An allusion to David controlling his reactions by counting to ten, a reference to his alleged stupidity, and a reference to his middle finger all in one picture. All that and fairly funny too. Well, we liked it.

Another Wordsearch was compiled, along the same lines as the first, but with the theme of Belgium. This time the answers included Belgian standards like Brussels, Ypres, chocolate, Atomium, Charleroi, Hoegaarden, Kriek, and Stella Artois; football related words like Anderlecht and Philippe Albert; and some slightly more obscure ones reflecting our own impressions and prejudices, such as sprouts, Poirot, bureaucrat, dull, tedious and boring.

Another quiz seemed in order too (answers p.229):

1 Which team has held the FA cup for the longest
   number of years?

2 The name of which English league club contains no
   letters from the word 'mackerel'?

3 Who won the Belgian league championship in the
   1999–2000 season?

4 Who missed the first penalty in the first ever penalty shoot-out?

5 Which club was Jean Marc Bosman signed to when he went to court to obtain a free transfer?

6 Who said "If my head had been a ball, it would have been in the back of the net"?

7 When QPR were due to play Sheffield United in the 1999–2000 season the game was postponed and rearranged for later in the season. Why?

8 What footballing record does David Gaultier of San Marino hold?

9 Which player has lost an FA cup final with three different clubs in the last 15 years?

10 Name all the English clubs to qualify for Europe at the end of the 1999–2000 season.

As we worked, we began to collect tales of slightly out of the ordinary experiences England fans had had at the previous evening's match. A Southampton fan rang to tell us about the tickets he'd *found* for the game. Four hundred of them, in fact. All in the name of the Portuguese FA. Sadly he'd found them too late, five minutes before kick-off, and dumped on the ground within the first cordon on the approach to the stadium. He expressed the opinion that this was a terrible waste, and the belief that there was probably England fans elsewhere in Eindhoven who would gladly have used them. Well, I could think of at least one.

Members of our team had been struck by the irony (they were always being struck by the irony of something or other, it was that sort of team) that in the Philips Stadium – home of the works team of the electronics company that gave the town its nickname of the 'City of Light' – in the stairwells of the Toys'R'Us stand, the lights didn't work.

One of the team, the very respectable international officer of the National Federation of Football Supporters Clubs Alan Bloore, had been prevented from taking into the stadium an offensive weapon. This story naturally gave rise to some bawdy comments about exactly how offensive his weapon could be, a situation not improved by his explanation that his 'weapon' had in fact been his half-time apple. This predictably gave rise to further ribald comments about this man of a certain age brandishing his shiny red cox in Toys'R'Us.

We found a cure for this ribald patch, in pride at how popular the first edition of our fanzine had been in the ground, with numerous reported sightings of people reading it at half-time. We ignored any suggestions that this popularity may have been exaggerated by the failure to materialise of the match programmes; we were told that match six of the tournament was a little too early to expect the printers to deliver by.

In the middle of all this creativity, we had more than half-an-eye on Charleroi and the looming Germany game. A couple of weeks earlier I had attended the annual conference of the German fan projects in Dusseldorf, a central theme of which had been their preparations for Euro 2000. The Germans were planning to run an embassy service similar to ours, but in their case the people running it were not volunteer fans, but social workers and youth workers seconded for a month from the fan projects which exist to work among young supporters at every major German club.

I had entered into what could be described as a gentleman's agreement with them that we would try to organise a fans' friendly football match between our embassy team and theirs.

Contrary to the recent trend, when I got back to England my colleagues did not all deny that I'd ever done any such thing. We thought that if we could generate some local media coverage we might be able to overcome the growing misconception among Belgian authorities that it would be impossible for a German and an Englishman to meet on the street without coming to blows. The idea had gone down well with both English and German Football Associations, who'd been very supportive, and with the British Embassy, and with the media people we'd sounded out about it. With everybody, in fact, except the Mayor of Charleroi, who we'd invited to kick off the game but who promptly banned it instead. Apparently he'd come under pressure from his local police chief who was worried that our match would attract a massive crowd (he'd clearly never seen us play), and rather than helping lighten the atmosphere would merely be another policing headache. We failed entirely to convince him that no-one would come, despite even offering to keep the whole game top secret, with any media coverage appearing only after the event. He may not realise it, but we did him a big favour by not telling anyone about his ban, as I'm sure that would have made banner headlines back home and in Germany.

So at a few days' notice we had a venue to organise, and we had a lot to talk to the Germans about. I asked them about their experience at their first game, which had taken place in Liege earlier on the same day as our game with Portugal. Their description of the German fans matched our experience (no, not the haircuts; they still maintained the usual crew cut/mullet differential); numerous, noisy, good-natured. The big difference had been in their treatment by the host authorities, which could be a sign of things to come. Unlike the Dutch, who started from an assumption that their visitors were all football fans with good intentions but remained ready and equipped to deal with any problems, the Belgians had seemed to proceed from an assumption that all German fans were potential hooligans, the peaceful ones being hooligans who hadn't got properly started yet.

The Germans had had a hint of what the attitude towards them might be when they received news of a mayoral pronouncement in Liege about special regulations introduced for the potentially explosive (eh?) Germany–Romania game. Knives and forks were to be banned from restaurants and bars in the city on match day.

This was the sort of decisive quick-thinking on security measures that would win respect for a mayor in the run-up to polling day. Having clearly identified a potential problem, he acted without hesitation to avert disaster. I sincerely hoped that he would not come to regret the limited nature of his decree. OK, the threat from knives and forks had been eradicated. But were they really the only dangers?

Would the Mayor be able to sleep at night if some poor innocent was the victim of a brutal spooning in his town centre? A spate of toothpick stabbings could lie heavy on his conscience in the months to come. Had he no idea of the havoc that could be caused by those little packets of pepper if they fell into the wrong hands? A mass outbreak of sneezing in the historic old town would not go down well with the electorate, especially given the possible collateral damage caused by Teutonic phlegm on passers-by. And the media could create a grossly distorted impression with vivid full-colour photographs of the aftermath of ketchup sachet battles. The Mayor of Liege must have heaved a huge sigh of relief when none of the German or Romanian fans showed any interest in anything other than the football. That and getting their hands clean after having to eat with their fingers all day.

We finalised the content we wanted in the fanzine after a

very long day but without any great difficulty, and sent it off to the printers by e-mail from the Eindhoven Fans' Embassy. I was ready for a day off by now, but I really should have known better. The next stage in the fanzine production process was to receive the proofs back from the printers for checking, and that was where we hit difficulties. I'm not technically sophisticated enough to know exactly what the problem was, but the combination of staying in a rural area with a weak mobile signal and trying to receive large files onto a laptop for checking was a very frustrating process. It appeared that we were able to receive 95% of the files several times over before losing the connection. Now I might have settled for checking 95% of the copy and taking a chance on the rest, but apparently it didn't work like that; if we didn't receive 100% of the files, we couldn't read any of them. The only alternative was to drive to the printers and do the proof-reading on site.

I could have done without the hassle, but it needed doing. I was a bit intrigued to meet the printers again and see how they were getting on. I'd met them a couple of weeks before the tournament when I came out to the Low Countries to, well, to find a printer. We were offering a slightly unusual deal. Challenging, in that all of the deadlines were very tight; we needed from them a twenty-four hour turnaround from receipt of copy to delivery of fanzines, which would be a tall order at the best of times. Add in the fact that they were dealing with a foreign language publication and that they had no advance knowledge where we'd be sending copy from (and neither did we), and there was plenty of scope for problems. To give them credit though, the firm we were using were fantastic. They couldn't have been more helpful, flexible and willing to work all hours. I got the impression they quite relished the challenge, and the quality of the stuff they turned out was excellent. Any mistakes in the production were all ours.

I had an idea we might have picked a good firm when they accepted with delight our proposal for payment. We didn't know exactly how many editions of the fanzine we would want to produce – we wanted one for each of England's games, but we couldn't be sure how many of them there would be – but we needed to finalise the budget, so I'd suggested a little gamble for them. I proposed that we pay them for four editions of the fanzine, come what may. If England were knocked out at the quarter-final stage, then we'd be quits. If we were knocked out at the group stage, after three games, then they'd hit lucky, and were paid for a fanzine they didn't produce. But if England got through to the semis, they'd have to provide us with a fanzine at no extra charge, in effect sponsoring it themselves. If England got to the final, we'd have to re-negotiate, but we'd be so happy we wouldn't really be worried about that.

The company – Thieme Deventer, for anyone considering ordering some printing work in the Netherlands and wanting to reward them with your custom – seized the challenge, and I really don't think it was because they were confident that England would get dumped out early. In fact after the Romania game they seemed genuinely disappointed not to be able to produce more, and were very critical of Phil Neville. But more of Phil Neville later.

The drive to Deventer and the couple of hours proof-reading, all on our day off, were to be compensated for by getting to use two tickets for the Sweden v Turkey game back in Eindhoven. Cathy and I were on our way back towards Eindhoven maybe an hour or two before kick-off when I got a phone call from Eurosupport. They told us that there had been some trouble in the centre of Eindhoven between Swedish and Turkish supporters, relatively small scale but nonetheless attracting some media coverage. The complication was that Dutch television had been carrying live pictures of the fighting accompanied by commentary saying that the fighting was carried out be 'English fans wearing Sweden shirts'. Could I please go and investigate?

I wasn't convinced that it was really my job to go and investigate anything, but as we were going to be in town anyway, I said I'd meet up with the Swedish fan coaches and find out a bit more, as it may become an issue. Sure enough, within ten minutes I'd received another call, this time from an English journalist, asking me to comment on reports of English fans fighting in Eindhoven.

We did indeed meet up with the Swedish fan coaches and the Dutch fan project workers who were working with them, and it turned out that they had been on the spot when the trouble started. They were highly amused when we told them what the Dutch TV had been reporting; the Swedes knew the fans involved as being from Gothenburg, and there had not been any English fans with them. The confusion may have arisen from the fact that the racists among the Swedes had chanted their racist abuse in English, the universal language of xenophobia.

Dutch television did later correct their story, but perhaps by then that particular piece of damage had been done. The Press Association reporter we bumped into on the way into the stadium had been as sceptical of the story as we had, so at least that particular episode did not add to the hysteria in the British press.

A magazine article I read after the tournament said that there had only been two poor games in the group stage. Naturally the Sweden–Turkey game was one of them.

Waterloo

Friday 16th June

KEVIN HAD PUT a lot of thought into his plans for the Germany game. Regardless of the result in Eindhoven, this was always going to be the big one. He had quite a personal history with the Germans, having himself been based there in his earlier years. And of course, every game between England and Germany had an extra significance.

Nobody is going to fall for this sort of deception again, I suppose, so it will already be clear that we're talking here about the fans' friendly football match against the Germans' Fans Embassy team. High noon was the kick-off time, and thanks to the assistance of both the FA and the staff of the British Embassy, we'd found a perfect venue. It had been noted by friends of ours in the FA in the course of some their own pre-tournament goodwill visits that the Mayor of Waterloo seemed more than happy to be associated with English football. Especially if English football attracted its usual amount of media interest, in this an election year in Belgium. (Not that I'm cynical or anything.)

And so it was that we ended up playing our game at the stadium of RRC Waterloo, a nice little ground of the sort that you'd expect to find in a small, affluent town where the main sport is rugby.

Aware of the advantages that can be gained by getting the upper hand psychologically, we decided to give the Germans a taste of their own medicine by arriving at the ground early and putting out towels down in the home dressing room. Sadly our other stratagem in the war of nerves didn't quite come off, as we failed to locate a Russian referee who would be available on a Friday lunchtime.

We were there early, but the police were there even earlier. It had been a condition of our holding the game that there was to be no advance publicity, in case that created another security problem requiring large-scale police resources. We were more than happy to comply, but the police came anyway, so that in a strange perversion of the usual proportions, there were more police present than spectators, but more players than police.

There was a lot of media interest, most of it very welcome, the exception being the arrival of a Sun photographer with a Page Three Girl, who tried to muscle in on the team photos. We didn't think her presence really contributed much to our message that football unites people across national boundaries. Kick-off was delayed for a few minutes though by all the other television and newspaper photographers who wanted pictures of our team, their team, mixed teams and of course the Mayor.

The game itself was refreshingly and surprisingly good. The Germans were no slouches, but we'd strengthened our squad by 'signing' one or two British media people we'd made contact with over the previous week. We didn't enquire too closely into the parentage or even grandparentage of one or two of them in case we didn't get the answer we needed. Suffice it to say we were pleased that none of the Germans raised any questions about the Scottish accent of GMTV's Alan Fisher who scored twice for England. Had they complained though, I had an ace up my sleeve; I happened to know that the Germans' own coach, a fan project worker based in Frankfurt by the name of Michael Gabriel, had himself played for Austria at under-21 level before his career was cut short by injury.

Lovely passing football we played, sweeping the ball through the German midfield but without enough sharpness in front of goal to convert all the chances. I thoroughly enjoyed myself, posing as a coach on the touchline, which basically involved walking up and down pointing and shouting. It must have sounded pretty convincing, at least to those who didn't understand a word I was saying, as a Belgian camera crew interviewed me later and asked which club I managed back home. Bless them.

We lost, in the end, by five goals to four, but it didn't feel like the end of the world at the time, and we joked with the Germans that we'd settle for them winning that game as we were going to win the real thing the following day. Ask any of us now, and we'll tell you we actually believed it too.

Charleroi

Friday 16th June

THE PLACE CHARLES II in Charleroi is not one of the great beauty spots of the Western world. An expanse of concrete, surrounded by buildings that in a generous mood you could say had character, always aware that it's a euphemism for 'not pretty'. On one side is the stone facade of the Hotel de Ville, or at least of the back end of it, as all traffic in and out of the building goes through doors on the other side. Around the square – as it came to be called, though it didn't have four sides or anything particularly regular about it – are bars, a couple of fast food restaurants, even a couple of shops and a bank. Narrow streets radiate away from it, some up towards the stadium, others downhill towards the lower town, but all seeming to leave the square rather than arrive at it.

Traffic circulates around the Place, in normal circumstances, like a roundabout, the centrepiece taking the form of the fountains. The very word 'fountains' conjures up an image of sculpted statues, perhaps of water nymphs or glorious heroes, but not in Charleroi. Here the fountains emerge from the flat plane of concrete, broken only by the glass covering the lights. The perimeter of the circle of fountains is marked by a line of concrete globes, each maybe twice the size of a basketball. Charleroi's idea of dressing the town for the festival of football consisted largely of dressing each of these balls, despite the fine weather, in a leather overcoat of hexagonal black and white patches, wittily giving them the appearance of . . . footballs. The metal pole that forms the centre of the circle of fountains has been adorned with a big . . . football.

It may have been an illusion caused by the nature of the Place, but the buildings all around seemed tall, the streets between them narrow. The ground floor facades of the bars and shops nearly all have balconies above them, and I would hazard a guess that in normal circumstances these balconies are rarely used. Arrive in Charleroi the day before the big match, however, and every one is occupied, by cameras, lights, microphones and monitors. Every media organisation worth its salt has booked itself a ringside box, a vantage point overlooking the square. The day before the big match, and reports are being filed about the media presence in the square, as if every crew has to demonstrate to their editorial team back home that they are not the only ones set up where nothing is happening. The media anticipation of a story is today the story itself.

Even early in the morning, when there are few people about in the square, I have a feeling that this is where things are going to happen. It takes me a while to identify the image forming in my mind, but eventually it becomes clear – this is an arena before the show begins. The stage is set, the camera crews are ready – more indeed than there will be in the stadium for the match itself – perhaps even the script is written. Sooner or later, this will be where the action is.

If the media organisations wanted a base in the square, the Fans' Embassy was no different. Only instead of a bar with a balcony, we had a van. We parked it outside the Hotel de Ville, where it could be easily seen, and began work. It was hot, so constant trips were made to the bar on the nearest corner, which it turned out had been colonised by the BBC. Well, not the bar exactly, though it sometimes seemed like it, but the room – and balcony, of course – above. The balcony gave a good view over the fountains and beyond, a safe place from which to film, and the room became the Radio Five Live studio for the next few days. My first visit to it confirmed my impression that these first floor balconies weren't usually used; the room seemed not to have been cleaned for a decade. It was one of those few places where the seemingly random dumping of a tonne of radio equipment and assorted cables could credibly be called an aesthetic improvement.

Down below, England were arriving. A trickle to start with, mostly people in search of tickets; most of those with tickets had apparently already consulted guidebooks to Belgium, which almost all extolled the virtues of everywhere else.

That's not to say that Charleroi doesn't have its plus points. Did you know that Napoleon and his troops had a meal there before marching on to Waterloo? Or that of all Belgian towns, Charleroi with its socialist traditions held out longest against the Nazis in the Second World War, for a total of 18 days? Or that this former coal-mining town known as the Black City can also claim to be the birthplace of the comic book? No, I bet you didn't. And you could spend the entire group stage of Euro 2000 without finding out either, unless you read our fanzine.

Although the big numbers of England fans did not arrive until the day of the game, there were enough people around to make the square look busy on the Friday. Most, unsurprisingly, were scattered around the bars, with the greatest concentration on the south side of the square. This group were still not particularly numerous, no more than a hundred certainly, but they were noisy, and as the day went on and the beer bellies got fuller, the singing got louder and the ominous choruses of 'No Surrender' more frequent.

The most surprising feature of Friday afternoon in Charleroi for me though was the complete absence of police from the square. OK, there weren't any big problems yet. But it didn't take a genius to see that the group on the south side were getting gradually bigger, noisier, and more threatening. Had this happened in Eindhoven, or even in London, I'm confident that a couple of coppers would have wandered across to them, chatted a bit, then dispersed them. Not by force, but a few words along the lines of 'Come on lads, it's getting a bit crowded here, can some of you move along to another bar please?' Early enough in the day and it would have been easily done. But the longer the day went on and the more the group got entrenched in place and in attitudes, the less likely it became that things would go smoothly.

I'd come across a situation like this once before, in the Old Port in Marseilles, 1998. A glorified mini-roundabout had been adopted by some England fans as the spot to spread out their flags, lie down and sunbathe. They'd been joined by more and more till there was no room left to lie down, so they'd logically all stood up. They had now become a small crowd and as the numbers swelled, some of the English fans began, inevitably and without malice, to spill over off the traffic island and into the road. There was still no hostility in the air, but even from our vantage point across the harbour, we could see a potential problem.

The solution was both obvious and simple – to me, at least. All it would take would be half-a-dozen coppers, but no more, to wander over and disperse the crowd. There might have been one or two choruses as they left, just to show there'd been no loss of face, but they'd have gone quietly enough, and peaceably. But there wasn't a policeman in sight, and no one tried to intervene. As a result, inevitably again, cars eventually had to start slowing down to avoid England fans in the road.

The singing got louder, so did the car horns. Somebody made a grab for a passing Tunisian flag, and missed.

In Marseilles the potentially difficult situation had been defused by a turn of events which verged on the surreal. From the side of the harbour passed an open-topped double-decker bus. From the top deck came the almost tuneful sound of the theme from *The Great Escape* played on brass instruments. It was *The Sun Bus*, News International's contribution to supporting the boys who support our boys. Star of the show was Melinda Messenger, who seemed to be conducting her own personal battle with gravity as she leant over the rail on the top deck, her broad grin above her substantial bodywork giving her the look of an inverted grand piano. Melinda and her able assistants were flinging white plastic bowler hats, decorated with the Cross of St. George and *The Sun*'s logo, into the melee below them. As the bus circled the crowded traffic island, it was greeted with cheers from English and Tunisians alike. Some of the less enlightened English fans began an impertinent chorus which seemed to express a desire to examine how well Ms. Messenger's cosmetic surgery scars had healed. White bowler hats were being put on everywhere. French grannies, English skinheads and Tunisian flagwavers, all united by a common absurdity of headgear. As quickly as they had developed, the beginnings of a fraught atmosphere evaporated on contact with *The Sun*.

Sadly in Charleroi the only sun making any impact was the hot one above, generating more thirst and frayed nerves. I could feel the atmosphere becoming increasingly tense by the hour, but still there was not a policeman in sight.

For the whole afternoon, the mood in the square was edgy, all because of the presence of a group of fans numbering less than a hundred. Across the rest of Charleroi, even in other bars in the same square, far greater numbers drank and chatted oblivious to any problem, in good spirits. Even the problematic hundred did not actually do anything apart from a few unpleasant chants, which none of the locals would have understood anyway. Good preventative policing would have dealt with the situation easily. But still there wasn't a single policeman in sight.

One obvious measure that could and should have been taken would have been to close the square to traffic, given the unusual numbers of people in it. Standard practice on big public holidays, and certainly the norm over the next few days. But all afternoon the traffic circulated, slowly, while fans spilled off the pavements into the road.

Later in the day, I witnessed the first of a few relatively minor incidents, any of which could have sparked major problems, all of which could have been prevented by even a token police presence.

First of all, two local youths, who couldn't have been more than sixteen-years-old, arrived on a scooter. They drove around the roundabout until they reached the group of England fans, where they stopped. The pillion passenger then very deliberately spat full into the face of one giant among the England fans.

I got the distinct impression that they consciously singled out this individual for their attention. Maybe there had been some earlier incident elsewhere involving him that I didn't know about. That's just my impression, and my speculation. Whatever prompted them to choose him for this provocation, it worked. While the big bloke was momentarily stunned, unable to take in what had just happened to him, the kids on the bike accelerated away as fast as their low-powered moped would go. The big bloke chased them and made a desperate lunge for the passenger, missing his shirt by inches. Had he been a fraction closer, he would have pulled him off the speeding moped onto the concrete, and who knows what would have happened next. I heaved a sigh of relief as the kids got away; the big bloke was understandably furious, but his anger seemed to calm down with his next pint.

The atmosphere seemed to subside for a while, which I now put down to the fact that a lot of people were watching France defeat the Czechs. By eight o'clock on this still, hot evening, the game was over and the French supporters were on the streets in a car cavalcade, bearing down on the square.

The next three incidents must have happened within the space of twenty minutes at most, although it seemed much longer at the time. Even at the end of this period, there was still not a single policeman to be seen in the square.

French cars were circling the square, blowing their horns and waving their national flags out of the windows. As they passed the south side, the England fans, now very drunk, were shouting at them and trying to grab the flags, but usually too clumsily to succeed. I noticed one car in particular; a very attractive young woman was standing with her head out of the sunroof, her tricolour hanging down the side of the car as her boyfriend (I presume) drove. I worried for her even as she passed me; sure enough her flag was grabbed, and she never stood a chance of winning the tug-of-war over it. There was a huge cheer from the England fans as they held their trophy aloft.

I could hardly believe what I saw next. The driver stopped his car, putting on the handbrake, and got out. I remember distinctly thinking to myself 'Don't do it, you idiot. It's only a bloody flag, this is an incident waiting to happen. Discretion is the better part of valour – she'll understand.' But it seemed like he wanted to be her hero. I hoped it wouldn't be posthumously.

As he approached the jeering England fans, hand out-stretched, something completely out of synch with my expectations happened. One of the England fans emerged from the group, shook the driver by his proffered hand and gave him back the flag, to a cheer from the crowd – a cheer more muted than the previous jeering, true, but a cheer nonetheless. I breathed out – a potential disaster averted, but still not a policeman in sight.

A few cars later, something else happened. I don't know who or what provoked it, if anything. What I do know is that from the crowd flew forward a plastic chair, into the road. (Flying patio furniture was to become quite a feature of Euro 2000 media coverage; this was my first recorded sighting. I can't help thinking in retrospect that this was quite an historic moment.) I felt instinctively that airborne seats were not a good sign, and I braced myself for worse to come. This had all the hallmarks of a trigger to something serious.

Once again I was amazed by the sequence of events. The chair didn't hit anything (which seems to be another characteristic of plastic patio furniture; for all its unlikely grace in the air, I think I've yet to see any hit its target. Perhaps it's not coincidence that so few of the missiles and projectiles designed by ballistics and aerodynamics experts have four legs, grooved seats for extra drainage and a cool but comfortable fan pattern on the upright back section.) Inevitably, someone stepped forward from the crowd – and picked it up, holding out the palms of his hands in an unthreatening, calming, apologetic gesture. Meanwhile others remonstrated with the chair-chucker, telling him to behave himself in an impromptu display of self-policing all the more necessary in the continued absence of any real police.

For a moment I thought maybe I'd misread the situation, that I'd been wrong to assume there was trouble brewing.

After all, this crowd may have been drunk, they may have been singing songs that I found objectionable, their language may have been indelicate, but they hadn't up until now done anything seriously wrong. Perhaps it would all pass without incident, they'd gradually disperse as the evening progressed.

That seemed a real possibility for a moment, but any last hopes disappeared within seconds. Cars were still cruising around the square, blowing horns and waving flags, when one vehicle, unobtrusive in comparison to the others, pulled to halt immediately beside the crowd. The driver got out, leaving his door open and the engine running. In his hand he held a weapon. I can't be sure exactly what it was – it may have been a club, or a torch, or a jack, or something similar – but it was wielded like a club. The driver walked quite calmly round the front of his car and straight to the crowd, who seemed nonplussed by his actions. He then raised his 'club' and began to batter one of the England fans – the same one who had been the target of the spitting earlier.

It can only have lasted a fraction of a second, but it was one of those slow-motion moments. The big bloke's head started bleeding immediately; his assailant turned and walked away – it was probably at very high speed, but it seemed like walking. There was a bit of a scuffle – he clearly hadn't got away fast enough – then he broke free and raced away across the square towards where I was standing, past me and away, pursued by half-a-dozen furious but slower Englishmen.

Part of this incident subsequently appeared on the now infamous BBC *Panorama* programme entitled 'England's Shame'. I don't know if it was a conscious decision in the editing process, or simply because they didn't get their camera rolling fast enough, but the footage they showed of this incident began with the scuffle and finished with the pursuit. It did not show the car very deliberately stopping, apparently unprovoked, in front of the crowd, or the driver getting out already armed. Nor did it show any of what happened next.

(Purely by coincidence, Paul Newman of the BBC happened to be broadcasting live when the aftermath of this incident was playing itself out behind him, creating or reinforcing the subliminal impression in viewers at home that this sort of thing had been going on all day.)

Again all of this seemed to me to happen in slow motion. I thought the car had been abandoned; it was where the driver had left it, engine still running, driver's door still wide open, driver disappearing at high speed on foot. As the pursuers gave up the chase and turned back, they turned their attention to the car. Someone stepped forward from the crowd and kicked it. I remember my confused reactions – the car's done for now, probably better that the car gets a kicking than the driver, no worse than the driver deserved – and then my surprise when a man got out of the front passenger seat, his palms raised in the same pacifying gesture one of the crowd had used earlier. Some of the crowd clearly weren't accepting his pleas of neutrality, others seemed hesitant, thrown by this unexpected attitude. As this passenger made his way cautiously around to the open driver's door, dodging attempted blows, a third man emerged from the back seat. This guy's gestures were not so conciliatory; in his hand he held an axe. He stepped towards the encroaching crowd waving it, they hardly surprisingly stepped back. Within a moment both men were back in the car, and the car was gone.

Everyone in the square seemed still to be in mid-gasp. For all the media presence there had been all day, it seemed that most of them had finished their shift for the day; it was now after eight-thirty in the evening, the packages for the evening news had already been filed. The crowd were now angry enough to retaliate, but there was no-one to retaliate against.

I wondered even then exactly what all that had been about. The initiative for what I'd seen had lain with the occupants of the car. True, the crowd had not been the type I'd have invited to meet my mam; they had been drinking heavily all afternoon, they'd been chanting, they were apparently absolutely determined not to give in to Irish Republicanism, they swore long and loud. There was an undercurrent of racism, though I don't recall on this occasion any overtly racist chanting. But none of that was justification for an armed attack, and there'd even been signs that this crowd were not intent on violence, they'd held back on one or two occasions when I wouldn't have been surprised if they waded in.

I could see that they wouldn't be particularly welcome visitors to a town, though. I could well understand that they would make ethnic minority communities feel uncomfortable, vulnerable, threatened. The men who had attacked them seemed to me to be of perhaps North African, Middle Eastern or Turkish origin; Turkish in the current shorthand of the travelling English racists, or even those English who had never had enough contact with any of these communities to make any distinction.

The evidence of my own eyes was that the England fans had not been much out of order, and had been victims of an unprovoked attack, yet in this instance their self-defence or retaliation would be what made the television screens. I still can't shake off the feeling though that there had perhaps been a bit of previous.

The attack by those in the car did not have the feel of a premeditated attack to start something. It seemed much more like a revenge mission, and could it really be coincidence that the same big bloke was singled out for attention on two separate occasions by locals? I suppose it's also possible that the two kids on the moped were just crackers, and had dared each other to mix it with the dangerous English they'd heard so much about. Perhaps they had then gone and told big brother about the bloke who'd tried to pull them off their bike. Possible, but I'm not sure. I'll never know.

Maybe the big bloke has something on his conscience – it's quite possible he was involved in some incident in a local restaurant the evening before, and was today getting his just desserts. But clearly there were a number of English fans in that crowd who'd just arrived. Their perception of the day was that they had had a good drink, done the things that England fans do, had been assaulted by locals, yet got the blame, and all the time there had not been a policeman in sight to protect them.

Half-an-hour later, there was no shortage of policemen in sight. Hundreds of them, all in riot gear, in paramilitary vehicles, including a water cannon, responding to reports of trouble in the square. Well, they'd been expecting it, they knew it was coming. The day had been quiet so far, they'd been in the barracks all the time, playing cards. Now they'd heard it had all started, they'd arrived in the square, and sure enough there they were, a crowd of England fans. Just like the papers had said.

Brussels

Friday 16th June

FOR THE REST of Friday evening, Charleroi was fairly quiet. Saturation policing in the square meant that people dispersed to other parts of the town in the hope of finding a bar or restaurant that didn't look as though it had just been, or was about to be, the epicentre of civil war.

Early on Saturday morning, the square was once again populated mainly by bar owners preparing for the new day – the bars would begin serving at 8.30 am – and media crews. I don't think I've ever felt like starting to drink alcohol at eight-thirty in the morning. There have been a few dissolute occasions when I've been *still* drinking at eight-thirty in the morning, but that's different. If I've ever had the sort of day ahead of me that wouldn't be adversely affected by alcohol consumption right at the start of it, then it wouldn't be the sort of day that I would want to start that early.

There were small numbers of England fans ready to start at that time of the morning, and one or two Germans too. As a result there was also a police presence, disproportionately large in numbers and fearsome in appearance. It seemed the Belgian police strategy knew two levels of operation, either of complete absence and inertia, or over-the-top in numbers and approach.

The rumour mill was already working overtime, generating many variations on the theme of one incident late the previous evening. The bare facts seemed to have been — I say facts, I didn't witness any of this, so I'm treating as facts only those elements of the story which were common to every version — that there was a small group of England fans drinking in one of the bars on the square in the early hours when a car pulled up outside. Men, by general consensus described as locals of Turkish or North African origin, got out, and began challenging the English to come and fight. When they did come out, a skirmish took place during which one of the England fans — later superfluously identified as an Ipswich fan — was stabbed. One of the locals drove off at speed, the others fled on foot.

Having established the bones of the story as reliable fact, listening to the development of the rumours became fascinating. Some of the variations were nothing more than the effects of loose narration, an informal Chinese whispers; others seemed to be consciously exaggerated or manipulated to serve a purpose. Within a couple of hours, the stories circulating included two English fans fighting for their lives in hospital as a result of a murderous attack by 'Turks'; shots having been fired, either by murderous 'Turks' or the police; policemen having been stabbed; the whole thing having been a warning attack as a prelude to mass carnage later in the day.

Even the BBC TV was broadcasting what it said was a Press Association report that the stabbed fan's condition had deteriorated to 'critical'. In fact I was subsequently told by British consular staff, who had visited him in hospital, that his wounds had never been serious, though he may simply have been lucky.

The consensus seemed to be that the English fans in this instance were the victims, more or less innocent. Though I must admit, of all the versions of the story I heard, none of them was a 'Turkish' version. It did not take much longer that day for us to receive several reminders that there is always more than one side to a story.

As the first of the England fans began to arrive in town from home, they brought with them the first copies of the day's English papers. Page two of the *Daily Mail* bore the headline *174 Arrested. England Fans Fight Police As Euro 2000 Violence Erupts*. The *Daily Star*'s report was headed *Riot Cops Wade Into English Yobs*. The *Express* had *England Fan Stabbed As Police Use Tear Gas On Rioters*. The *Mirror* carried a full-page photo feature on one particularly zealous Belgian undercover policeman and his 'one-man war on English louts', all captioned *Belgian Robocop 5, Thugs 0*. (By the way, just a thought – this policeman bore a striking resemblance to Jean-Claude Van Damme, and he was Belgian. Can this be coincidence, or are they perhaps related? Or was it in fact J-C himself, earning a few extra francs moonlighting?)

The others all continued in similar vein. I could just about recognise what I had witnessed in Charleroi from the press accounts – although of course the reports concentrated exclusively on the '200 drunks' causing problems, instead of the rather greater numbers who had just got on with enjoying the day. I suppose that's inevitable; a 'lack of incidents' doesn't really constitute a news story. Still, it was one more case that fuelled the impression that wherever England fans are mentioned, there's trouble.

From what I read though, the events in Brussels, to which a lot of the papers referred, seemed to have been more serious. Certainly the arrest figures were high at 174. For the first time reporters were having to get to grips with the distinction between 'administrative detention', which under Belgian law does not require any offence to have been committed and which made up 139 of the 174 'arrests', and real arrests, which accounted for the other 35.

I did have the advantage of having direct access to a first-hand account of what had gone on in Brussels, in the form of a group of embassy volunteers who'd been there. It turned out that they had managed to spend several hours in the capital the previous evening without witnessing any acts of violence themselves – so much for the idea that the whole city had been plunged into anarchic street fighting for hours on end.

That's not to deny that there had been trouble. Anyone who has since seen the *Panorama* programme which was broadcast immediately after the England – Romania game will have seen the footage shot by their undercover cameras of English thugs – plus the odd Welshman, it would seem – screaming racist abuse, bellowing chauvinistic chants, throwing punches and missiles, damaging property, and generally being anti-social.

Our embassy team members did come across some of these individuals later staggering drunkenly about urging 'England' to 'stand together' and 'get the Turkish bastards'. Yet for all the talk previously of the 'zero tolerance' approach to be expected, none of the police they passed did anything about this. Surely this was just the sort of racist, anti-social behaviour they'd been planning to target?

As the evening progressed, it had become increasingly clear that 'targeting' was not a particularly appropriate word to describe Belgian policing methods. Targeting implies, after all, focusing on a particular troublemaker or group of trouble-makers and singling them out for attention. We soon learned that far from dealing with individual examples of unacceptable behaviour and isolating the perpetrators from the rest of the England fans, the Belgian police made little or no attempt to differentiate between those intent on trouble and the ordinary supporters drinking in the vicinity. At first this had meant hardly any police presence; later it became apparent that the Belgian authorities were of the opinion that *all* England fans were trouble, and thus should all be treated accordingly.

Our team members in Brussels first became aware of this when they talked to England fans whose friends had been caught up in trouble earlier in the day, and had been arrested. One lad called Paul explained that he alone of his mates had been spared arrest, and then only because he'd been having a tear gas-induced asthma attack at the time.

In the hope that our man Jim's fluent French might help clarify why Paul's mates had been detained, they went to the police station to ask where they were being held and what was likely to happen next. Fluent French didn't prove necessary however as the Desk Sergeant's English was very clear. It went something like this: 'He's going to be deported and if you don't fuck off, you will be too.'

A lot of people at home watching the television footage of some of the worst elements of the thugs doing what they do in the name of supporting England will have come to the conclusion that they got just what they deserved at the hands of the Belgian police. Having come across some of these characters at close quarters myself, I wouldn't disagree. Genuine supporters don't want them around. Genuine supporters want rid of them so we can get on with enjoying the football.

The problem though is that the Belgian police's approach doesn't simply fail to get rid of these people. It actually makes that process harder. I believe that if you want to cleanse England's support of the racist thugs, the first step is to isolate them from the rest, by making everybody else feel consciously different from them. One way might be to build the confidence among the others to assert their standards and values in supporting England. It might be to create a climate where anti-social behaviour is unacceptable. There's scope for a useful debate about this. But one thing that won't help, that will in fact be counter-productive, will be to treat everyone the same, as if they're all thugs. Far from isolating the trouble seekers, this gives them somewhere to hide, and alienates the others – not from the thugs, but from the authorities.

As soon as the arrest figures from Friday night in Brussels were published, the Belgian police were moved to explain that only 35 were likely to face any charges. This did not affect any of the newspaper headlines. It was clear however to anyone who had experienced a tournament abroad that the much larger figure of those subject to 'administrative detention' must include many fans who had been guilty of nothing more than being in the wrong place at the wrong time.

The FSA subsequently collated a dossier of evidence from such fans, which we used to illustrate the unreliability of lists of those detained provided by the Belgian authorities as a basis for banning from future tournaments. To debar these individuals from travelling abroad in future would be to compound the injustice they had already endured and which had ruined their Euro 2000 experience.

Some of the testimony of these fans is reproduced here. These statements are given in full; any resulting repetition serves to underline their authenticity, and to convey the fact that these were not unfortunate but isolated individuals. What we had here were significant numbers of victims of indiscriminate policing.

Peter is a 39 year old Computer Consultant and
lives in London with his girlfriend and their 9 month
old baby:

*I have supported Tottenham all my life and have had a
season ticket on and off over the years. I enjoy many sports,
have played football regularly since I was ten and I am also
a qualified table tennis coach.*

*On Friday [June 16th] at around 8am, I left for Waterloo
station to get the Eurostar to Brussels, to enjoy a weekend
away having a few drinks, a bit of a sing-song, a laugh
and a joke and to watch some class football in Bruges and
Charleroi.*

*We chose to stay in Brussels because it was a mid-point
from the two matches we were to attend. We set off after
a full breakfast on the Eurostar and arrived in Brussels at
around 13.30. We booked into our hotel, the room was a
bit small for five of us but we would only be sleeping there
so at around 16 pounds each and so close to the town we
couldn't complain. We went to the France v Czech Republic
game in Bruges and had a great time. The football was of
a high standard but it was a shame to see a team with the
Czech Republic's class go out at such an early stage in the
tournament.*

*On the way back two of my friends went to Ostend to see
if they could get a ticket, as we were one ticket short for the
England v Germany game the following day. We arrived
back in Brussels at around ten in the evening and decided
to have a couple of drinks and something to eat.*

*At one bar there were a few songs sung by the English
fans. One or two of the songs were a bit racist so we obviously
didn't join in. With my skin colour not one supporter was
intimidating towards me even though I could have been*

thought as of ethnic origin. I didn't have an English shirt on and neither did any of my friends, so it would have not been obvious I was English without speaking to me.

We met up at a bar with our friends at around 1.20am and carried on having a bit of a sing-song. We were not drunk just a bit merry. At times the bar was noisy with lots of singing but you expect that when people are enjoying themselves. We were chatting and having a laugh and a drink with French, Dutch and locals.

At around 2am about thirty English fans decided to wander off down the road to look for some Turkish supporters to sing at/shout at/fight with, whatever was on their mind, and it looked like it may get a bit ugly. As they were going away from where we were drinking we didn't think anything of it and stayed there.

Literally seconds later we could see police chasing them back towards the bar, at this point the owner shouted that the bar was closed and proceeded to shut the door. As I was near the door the sensible thing to do seemed to be to stay in the bar as the riot police were indiscriminately beating anyone in front of them. I moved to the back of the bar away from the windows, sat down with my friends and continued to chat. We thought that was the end of it, but how mistaken we were.

The police arrested anyone outside and took them off in vans with sirens blaring. Next they ordered the bar owner to open up and came in with batons to remove everyone. Once outside they put electrical cable grips around our arms behind our backs, then made us all sit in a line on the floor. We called it later 'Gap Band' formation though it wasn't funny at the time. It was just like a scene from Robocop and we did wonder when we were going to wake up from the nightmare.

One by one we were taken off to coaches and most of our valuables and our belts were taken from us and put in bags matching the sticky labels on us, I presume mine said 'Prisoner 952'. Then with sirens blaring and lights flashing we were taken to the Gendarmerie where we were to be held. It turned out that it was full, so next we were driven in the same fashion to the old Heysel stadium (though we obviously didn't know any of this at the time).

Near the stadium a temporary police cell had been set up in a fire station. We were unloaded van by van into what can only be described of as a cage. Some of the supporters were shouting as the cuffs had been put on too tight and their hands were turning blue, but the police just ignored their pleas. Eventually they did cut off the cuffs and by this time around 35 to 40 supporters were in the cage, which was attached to the wall. The dimensions were about 10 feet by 12 feet and 10 feet high so it wasn't possible for us to all sit down at the same time. We didn't have a clue what was going on so we just chatted and tried to keep anyone getting annoyed as calm as possible. There was a French, a Dutch and a Belgian supporter amongst the group. Any questions we asked the police were answered with a shrug of the shoulders and either 'we are just obeying orders' or 'I do not understand.'

One of the men urinated and excreted in his trousers, so as you can imagine after four or five hours it was not pleasant in there. I was thankful for the small mercy that my sense of smell is so bad. Eventually they gave us some water and let us out one by one to use the toilet. As the morning broke with spirits well down, someone started whistling 'Always look on the bright side of life' and it was quite funny for a five-minute spell as a few of us sang the verses in between the chorus.

However again one by one we were taken in to give all our details; this must have taken a good couple of hours if not longer. At around 8.30am it was my turn, I gave my details and asked if it was an offence to have a drink in a bar in Belgium. The reply I got was not satisfactory but it was made obvious by the body language that I should only take it further if I fancied them taking it further with me, I think you know what I mean. The answer I got was 'I was English and in the wrong place at the wrong time'. I was then returned to the cage.

Some of the police were complete bastards and others were in comparison mildly sympathetic but again said they were 'just obeying orders'. During the time in there they stood in front of us eating drinking and laughing. After realising it was one bloke's birthday, they started singing 'Happy Birthday' to him from their offices, my turn tomorrow probably. Every now and again some would stand around banging batons and lowering the garage type door of the building. The worst part of it was not knowing what was likely to happen next.

One chap who spoke fluent French demanded to know what was going on and refused to return to the cage when taken to the toilet. He was put in a cell very roughly and quickly. We eventually asked if a spokesman could talk to whoever was in charge and he was allowed out. Again we found out later that they just put him in another cell for a couple of hours; he didn't speak to anyone.

Eventually we were given a box of Indonesian waffles which when smelt almost made me throw up, but as I didn't know how long we would be there I forced a couple of mouthfuls down and threw the rest back in the box, as did everyone else.

At around midday some of us were cuffed and our

valuables were returned. I think I would have preferred something to eat or a decent drink. We were then put on a coach with the same cage-type grills on and taken, so we thought, to our hotels so we could be escorted in to collect our belongings. After about an hour the coach was pretty hot and again we asked for drinks and food but were met with shaken heads. About four or five of the group managed to visit their hotels and get their stuff yet the cuffs remained on. One chap was allowed out of the coach to be sick and it was at this point that the police decided to get some water for us.

Next thing we knew we were being hurried back to the Fire Station where the cage was and told that the rest of us would have to leave without our gear as the plane was waiting. We were astounded to see the rest of those arrested still in the cage. At least we had been out for a short while. At the station, one by one, we were made to sign a document written in mostly French/Flemish, saying that we agreed we had committed offences and we agreed to being deported. After what had been happening, some of us signed just to get home while others refused. However it seemed to make no difference as to how we were treated.

Again the shutters were open and closed. It was at this point that some of us realised that they were trying to provoke us so that they could wade in and subsequently have something to charge us with. The word was passed around to everyone to stay calm. By this time a few more of the police seemed to be increasingly sympathetic towards us and tried to reassure us. As some of us had our valuables, mobile phones included, we were able to phone the British Embassies in different countries, but were told nothing could be done. Fortunately everyone remained calm bar the odd shout of anger.

Next, everyone was taken in the coach again, just like

criminals, to the airport. We waited there for most of the afternoon and evening watching three planeloads of fans being flown off. We were told some had come from Charleroi that day and one load were German fans/thugs. About 95% of the supporters were okay but bruised faces, arms and legs suggested we were the lucky ones.

One lad had his arm in a sling and when he could not sit on the floor the police pushed him down with a baton, watching him land on his broken arm. Because our group had not resisted or voiced too much anger, the police seemed to realise that our group had been treated unfairly. They were speaking to us in a friendlier manner and trying to get us relevant information.

At around 11pm we were taken to the Gendarmerie. The result of the game had filtered through to us, but by this time it didn't really mean anything at all.

The police who had been with us throughout the day thought all the people on our coach should be released — maybe because we had now been held for almost 24 hours. The person in charge would not listen, however, and seemed to suggest that they had been given orders to deport us no matter what. The confusion angered them but they passed us over to the Gendarmes to be put in a cell, which was extremely basic, all concrete, but with a lot more space. In comparison to the cage it felt like a palace. We had been told that we would be fed but as with all the other promises no food materialised, only more water. We could hear people in other cells were not so lucky as the sounds suggested some of them were being beaten about.

After about half-an-hour we were taken back to the military airport. Eventually one by one, each of us with a plain-clothes policeman for company, we were put onto a very basic and noisy military Hercules jet to be flown home, but as air traffic control was down it would be to Manchester not Stansted.

Some people were glad of this, others not so, but we had been promised transport back to London if we required. We assumed that as we had been deported we would be arrested in England and charged but at least we could get some sort of justice. We learned from the plain-clothes police during the flight that it was their sixth flight of the day, with one more to come. We realised that there must have been around 450 fans picked up each night and the English police/Government must have had some idea what was going on.

When we arrived at Manchester the cuffs were taken off, and we went through a temporary passport control. Details were asked about how we had gone to Belgium, who we had gone with, where we were staying and who we supported. We were then sent through the airport and told we were free to go home. There was, however, no transport, quelle surprise.

The game I have played and loved for 30 years of my life put me in this position. I had tickets for more games as well as the final but I simply couldn't care what happened for the rest of the tournament. England winning, losing or drawing means nothing to me.

I hope time will heal my feelings and I return to playing and watching but at this moment I just do not know.

Millwall fan Paul Nightingale was in Brussels with two friends, both called Andrew:

We arrived in Brussels around lunchtime on Friday June 16th, and found a hotel near the centre of the city. We then went for a drink in O'Reilly's, an Irish bar, but decided to leave after about an hour and head towards a quieter bar to watch the match between France and the Czech Republic. After the game all the French fans left the pub; a short time after this we heard a lot of commotion from the main street outside the bar. The three of us decided to stay in the bar to avoid any disturbances.

After around half-an-hour we decided to find somewhere to eat. We remembered having seen an Italian restaurant in the main square and decided to head towards it. There was a large police presence blocking two of the entrances to the square, so we decided to go into a small bar nearby to keep out of the way. We were talking to a few other English supporters who had also done the same.

Suddenly several dozen England supporters ran into the bar after being attacked with CS gas by the police we had seen outside. At this point the mood inside turned into panic as the riot police approached the glass-fronted bar. The door was opened and a CS gas canister was thrown in without warning. We were unable to breathe and the gas got into my eyes so badly I could not make out the exit.

After eventually finding my way out of the bar I was forced to lie face down on the dirty street. After a few minutes the police then dragged me to my feet and made me sit in a line with all the other supporters. I then saw my friend Andrew being taken by a policeman to a van. I tried to explain that I would like to go with him, but they did not (or did not want to) understand.

After about five minutes they then put us into a van and drove us to what appeared to be a local police station, which had an open area. It was surrounded by blocks of flats, from which lots of people were taking photos. After two hours and without explanation we were again herded into police vans and driven for about fifteen minutes, nine men in the back of a van designed to seat six. I would also like to add that we were still handcuffed at this point. The van eventually arrived at a prison where we were supposed to have a form filled in for us saying why we had been arrested, who we were and where we were from, as well as what time we had been arrested. However the officer who filled in mine had obviously had enough of filling them in and decided that he would just put my name and nothing else. He then took me to sit outside the prison where about 200 English were.

During the six hours we sat there around another 75 people were brought in and I would add that they were not all English. Then the police realised that the handcuffs were too tight on most people and that they needed to loosen them. They then started to move us off. Being one of the first to move I quickly found out that they were expecting us to sleep in a horse-training centre, the floor of which was made of fibre glass (not very comfortable). After a further six hours we were eventually moved into the prison. On entering we were asked to take off belts and shoelaces. We were then asked to sign a form. When I asked what I was signing for I was told to just sign. Eventually after asking three times the lady told me in almost perfect English that it was only for the possessions I had on me. I then asked why I had been arrested to which she said she did not know. I asked if she could find out; she said 'what does it matter?' I found this comment unacceptable. We were also told that the British Consulate would not be coming to see us, as there were too many of us.

We were informed that we would be going home in three hours. We had our photo taken and were placed in a small cell (18 men in a cell that was supposed to hold only six). Most of us did not get a blanket and had still not had any offer of food or water. This I am sure is completely against *all human rights and even if it is not, it is unbelievable in an EU country.*

Eventually some water in a plastic bag was given to us but this tasted stale. They then brought us some waffles. We were told on numerous occasions that we would be going home soon and on two occasions we were woken up to be told this. All turned out to be false alarms. We were eventually moved upstairs to a larger cell. Soon more people were brought in bringing the total number of us in the cell to 32.

After 42 hours I was eventually sent home via a Belgian army plane to London Stansted where we had to give our details and have our picture taken for the British police. After being escorted onto a train to Liverpool Street station we were left with no money and no way to get home. Luckily I live in London and was able to get a cab and pay at the other end.

The main points that I would like to bring to your attention are:

- *The fact that there was repeated misinformation passed on to us.*

- *The fact that we were held for 42 hours without being charged. Belgian law says that you can only be held for 12.*

- *The fact that in 42 hours no exercise was offered and toilet and washing facilities were only available during the last four hours.*

- *The fact that no hot food was offered. Water was hard to come by. The only food given to us was out-of-date sandwiches and three waffles — not enough for a young child, let alone a fully-grown man.*

- *Lack of blankets.*

- *The fact that we were not allowed to make a phone call home which caused a lot of problems for my family (especially as my friend arrived home fourteen hours before me!).*

All the above points I'm sure have to be addressed. I would have expected better treatment than this if I had been a mass murderer let alone being an innocent football supporter. One further point was the way the police were spotted laughing at the way some of us looked. This simply added insult to injury.

Steve Holt is a Manchester City fan living in Winchester. He travelled to Euro 2000 with his brother Lee and three friends.

I have been watching England games at home and abroad for over ten years. I am a member of the England Members Club and had tickets for all three group games, along with vouchers for the Quarters, Semis, and Final if England had progressed.

I am also the Secretary/Chairman of the Winchester Branch of the Manchester City Centenary Supporters Association which now has over 50 members in the Hampshire area, and I'm a regular attendee at City games home & away. I have never been involved in football violence with either City or England.

We were all arrested in a Brussels bar near to where

there had been trouble involving England fans. Some of those involved in the incident came into the bar and the riot police decided to surround the building and arrest EVERYONE inside which incidentally also included a France supporter in a France shirt, two Sweden fans and a Belgian. They were released from custody after about three hours once the police came to realise they were not English.

At the time of arrest we were handcuffed by means of plastic ties behind our backs and made to sit in the road in single file. We were then herded onto police coaches. At this point I was separated from my friends. The coach I was on was driven to a jail. After a while outside the gates of the jail we were told the place was full and were driven to somewhere which looked like a fire station near to the Heysel Stadium.

Once there we were stripped of our possessions and put into a cage which I estimated to be approximately sixteen feet by ten feet. There were close to 40 of us inside. There was no room to sit down inside this cage. We were angry at our wrongful arrest and demanded to know what was happening. One at a time we were taken into the office part of the building. We were asked for our name, address etc and had our photographs taken before rejoining the group back in the cage. My request to make a telephone call was declined. I had hoped to call the British Embassy in Brussels. The number was in my wallet, having been supplied by the England Members Club in case of emergencies including arrest.

I should point out we were arrested at about midnight on Friday June 16th.

Back in the cage we waited and waited and were eventually given a couple of bottles of tap water between us at about 6am.

A few of the detained began to ask for some food at this

time. We were eventually given a disgusting waffle each at about 10am. I didn't see anyone actually eat a whole one!

About four hours later we were at last given some information. An officer appeared from the and told us that we would be taken to our hotels to collect our things and then taken straight to the airport where a plane would be waiting to take us back to England. We again protested our innocence but to no avail. I began to feel really depressed when I finally realised that I wouldn't be watching the game against Germany later that evening. I had been saving up for and looking forward to this fixture for months.

The next step at approximately 2pm was to give the police the name of our hotels. The people who had hotels in central Brussels, including myself, were handed our possessions back and led (handcuffed) onto a waiting coach. We arrived at the first hotel and one of the guys was taken to his room to gather his things. We visited two more hotels and were then told there was no more time. We then returned to the cage where the others who were not staying in central Brussels were still detained.

As I had my possessions back, I managed to get a photograph of the cage without the police noticing. One at a time the English detainees were led back into the offices and were asked to sign a document written in French. Some signed in the belief that it would speed up their release but I personally refused to sign, as I didn't have a clue what I was supposed to be signing for. I guessed it was some kind of admission of guilt.

After everyone had been given the chance to sign we were put back onto coaches and driven with sirens sounding to an airfield where about five Belgian Air Force planes were lined up. I would estimate we arrived at this airport at about 5pm.

We were under the impression that we would be put on the next available flight back to England but this wasn't the case at all. Whilst we waited, we witnessed six coachloads of fans arrive AFTER us and be driven straight to a plane ready to take them home.

Some five hours later we were asked to get back on the coach and we were driven back to Brussels and the jail that had been full the previous night. After much confusion we were led to a large cell and were handed a bag of water. We had still not had anything to eat other than the first bite of a dry waffle. We had now been held in custody for over 24 hours.

We remained in the cell for about an hour and were then led back onto coaches and driven to the airport once again.

This time we only had to wait a further half-an-hour or so before being led onto the airforce carrier plane. There was a policeman or policewoman on the plane for every Englishman. We were STILL handcuffed for the takeoff, the journey and the landing. Surely anyone with any sense would realise that being handcuffed throughout a flight is a very dangerous practice.

We arrived at Manchester Airport at about 3.30am local time and were finally uncuffed as we disembarked. We answered some questions for the immigration officials and the Manchester Police before being set free to make our way home. I now found myself over 200 miles from home without my passport, any English money, my house key and the clothes I had taken on holiday. One of the guys I had spent the last day or so with kindly paid for a coffee and something to eat for me at the airport 24-hour cafe.

After saying our farewells I managed to contact a friend of mine in Manchester and told him of my predicament. He kindly picked me up from the airport and I had a few hours sleep on his sofa. This was the first sleep I had managed since waking at 8am on Friday (48 hours ago). From his flat I found out the train times to Winchester and the cost. He lent me £100 to pay for the train (£51) and to buy some refreshments. After a train delay, I arrived back home at 9.30pm on Sunday June 17th.

I managed to text a message to another friend of mine who kindly diverted his journey to Charleroi to collect our bags from our hotel in Brussels. I now have these bags back in my possession, but have since found out that one of my friends had £150 sterling missing from his wallet. Another had 10,000 Belgian Francs missing from the safe box in his room and my mobile phone charger was also missing from the room. My brother who was staying in another hotel had his credit card used fraudulently whilst he was in custody.

One of the lads actually lives and works in Amsterdam and a group of us stayed at his house for the first five nights of the tournament. Some of our belongings, which we didn't take to Brussels, are still at his house.

I have spoken to him since I arrived home and was told that even he was deported back to England! He obviously had problems convincing the authorities that he wanted to return home as they thought he was returning for the football.

Finally on Sunday June 24th, the local police came around to my house to tell me that I was banned from entering Holland & Belgium until after the July 2nd. This proved embarrassing with my neighbours looking on. I am very angry at the way all England fans are tarred with the same brush when we travel abroad. To be fair, the Dutch police were fantastic. They mixed and joked with the English supporters in Eindhoven and certainly were not out to show how forceful they could be.

Steve Merchant had similar experiences in Brussels, and sustained a broken arm at the hands – or batons – of the riot police:

On Friday June 16th two friends and I arrived in Brussels looking forward to enjoying a convivial atmosphere in which to enjoy the Euro 2000 tournament.

Leaving our hotel at 8.30 pm we arrived in the main square in Brussels and sat outside a bar enjoying an early evening beer. The atmosphere inside & outside of the bar was very relaxed and friendly with all concerned looking forward to the upcoming match with Germany.

Suddenly, we were confronted with the sight of many English fans being chased into the square by the Belgian police, some of whom entered the bar outside which we were situated.

Despite the fact that it was obvious that the people outside the bar were not involved in any of the fracas, the police proceeded to physically assault fans indiscriminately.

Seeing what was occurring, my two friends & I decided it would be wise to leave the area and proceeded to try to leave the square only to find all exits blocked by police.

Closing in on us the police began beating us to the floor with their truncheons and in my case my left arm was broken. I was handcuffed and then forced to lay face down on the pavement.

After some minutes I 'dared' to raise my head to ascertain what was happening around me and was dealt another blow by the policeman to my right shoulder. I was then escorted to another area in the square where other English fans were being held.

Despite my protestations that my arm was hurting, especially as by now I was handcuffed, it was some three hours later that a nurse was summoned and I was sent to hospital, though effectively under armed guard.

Please remember that I had been guilty of absolutely no offence to warrant such treatment, which amounted to legalised thuggery by the Belgian police.

As well as suffering physical abuse, the only way the police communicated to us was using a succession of swear words all in perfect English!

I have to say that the medical staff at the hospital were very nice and seemed genuinely concerned with my predicament. However, once my arm had been set in plaster, I was escorted by police car to a detention centre where other English 'hooligans' were being held.

On arrival, I was informed that I would be held there for approximately two hours prior to being released, as it was accepted that I hadn't actually committed any offence and was being held as a precautionary measure.

In fact I was to spend the next 17 hours in custody and during that time all I was given to eat was a stale waffle and some water to drink.

The police within the detention centre did have some sympathy with our plight and described the riot police that had broken my arm as 'crazy'.

During my time in the centre I was in a lot of pain and was very shivery, probably as a result of my injury. I heard many stories of men of all ages being subjected to similar thuggery and some youngsters were very frightened as to what would happen to them. Fortunately, I did have a mobile phone and was able to let my parents know what was happening — many others asked to phone home but their requests were rejected.

Eventually, at approximately 3.00 am on Sunday June 18th I was put on a military plane and flown back to Manchester. For every prisoner, the plane contained one *police officer which when you consider that we were all handcuffed, was way over the top!*

This whole experience was a personal nightmare for me especially as, during my 21 years, I have never been in any trouble with the police.

I would like to add that I have no sympathy with real football hooligans and of course understand that many people arrested were done so deservedly. However, as a basic human right, it is totally wrong that a police force can ever be justified in the savage attacks being inflicted onto people like myself and indeed many others whose only crime was being in the wrong place at the wrong time.

Back in the UK I had to arrange for my Brussels hotel to pack the bags of myself and my friends and arrange for them to be sent to my home in England, all at our own expense.

What makes me mad is the stories emanating from politicians, UEFA officials etc that '800 plus football hooligans have been deported from Belgium for acts of violence'. Such a figure is a total fabrication. The old adage, — 'there are two sides to every story' has never been more true.

In other words: Not everyone deported from Belgium was a football hooligan.

37 year old Joseph Murray from Birmingham was also hurt by police actions:

I'd been at another bar when some trouble started, (people, Turks I think, throwing bottles at the English) so my friends and I left. We were walking towards some bars nearer to our hotel for safety. Suddenly some police came charging up the road and arrested everyone. I was thrown to the floor and a policeman hit me firstly on the hand with a baton. I received a broken bone in my hand, broken ribs and stitches in my face. I was taken to hospital by the police, where I was x-rayed and a plaster placed on my hand. I was then taken to a prison complex or police station and put in a cell with about 50 others in the early hours of Saturday morning. I was released in the early hours of Sunday morning, returned to my hotel, and came home. I was off work for eight weeks and am still in considerable pain.

One message the FSA received was from someone who was not deported, but his story was if anything even more disconcerting. At least the others had a clear recollection of what had happened to them – which is more than you could say for Carl Blissitt:

I was not deported from Brussels in Euro 2000 but at the time I wished I had been. A day that started as a carnival experience quickly turned into a nightmare. After witnessing Belgian police trapping many English fans (many of them my friends) with military style tactics I decided that the best idea was to keep out of the way and make my goal of Charleroi the next day. Though incensed at seeing with my own eyes police and Turkish fans joining forces to beat English fans I found a quiet bar across the road from my hotel, the Ibis.

At 1.00am in the morning all seemed quiet. A group of about 15 to 20 English fans were finishing drinks in a bar near the Grand Market Place when we were forcefully attacked by Belgian police, I can only imagine for being English. The next few minutes are a bit of a blur. All I remember was blood running down my head, being forced into a van and then being blindfolded. In a situation like this you talk to yourself in your head and I was telling myself that, even though I was blindfolded, they must be taking me to the hospital. Wrong!!

When they removed me from the vehicle, still blindfolded, I could hear people speaking angrily and loudly. Every time I lifted my head, as the blood poured down my face, I was beaten around the body with batons. The worst was yet to come. I could now feel them lifting my T-shirt and I started to struggle in fear.

At this point they briefly lifted my blindfold and I could see paramedics there who also in my own opinion looked to be in fear. They were being told to inject me in the back. This may well have been for medical reasons but something told me this was not right. It was obvious I had been drinking and I did not fancy trusting people who had just beat me and blindfolded me. After being held down by many people, I was indeed injected in the back. I was then blindfolded again and occasionally beaten at their will.

I was suddenly moved and put back into a vehicle. The doors opened and I was flung into the street blindfolded. Not bothered about grazed knees from being thrown from the vehicle I removed my blindfold to find I was nowhere I recognised. People were still hanging around on street corners in the early hours of the morning. They did not seem friendly and I started to run in fear. I just kept running even though my legs had been beaten. I eventually found my hotel at 10.30am on Saturday morning. I entered my hotel room to find one of my friends asleep; he had left for bed the previous night just before my nightmare began. The phone rang and it was my other friend who had been deported, asking us to take all his bags with us.

The next few days, because of the big gash I had on my forehead, many people asked me how I had been injured and by whom. I started to think, as I was never arrested, that maybe it was not the police but a gang who had kidnapped and beaten me. Surely a European country like Belgium's police could not have done something so barbaric? I returned to England to explain to bosses and family how I had received my injury and that I was innocent and not a hooligan. I got the feeling that they probably did not believe my story as when I was telling it even I thought it sounded far-fetched.

A colleague told me of a programme about Euro 2000 on Trevor McDonald's Tonight. *So I set up my video recorder and watched. There I was, covered in blood being manhandled by BELGIAN POLICE. The only consolation for me of seeing these pictures is that they prove my story.*

I am shown being arrested and covered in blood although records will show I was never arrested or deported. So if they have pictures of me with the police, what did they do with me? Although this proved my story I was still upset about the fact that I was shown on a programme made to show English hooliganism during Euro 2000. I emailed Trevor McDonald to complain about being shown and the implication of being branded a hooligan, thug and animal. I received a reply from the deputy editor of Tonight *which incensed me. It says that the Brussels mayor had conceded that the tactics his officers used would result in some 'collateral damage'. I suggest that the Brussels police are the animals, not the innocent English football supporters.*

Judging by their words, none of the people quoted above fit the stereotype of the racist thugs that undoubtedly do infest England's away support. That hooligan element is a minority; there may be scope for argument about exactly what proportion, but they are undoubtedly a minority. Fans like Peter, Martin, Paul, Steve, Joseph and Carl are much more typical of the average England fan, yet clearly from the way they were treated, no attempt was made to differentiate between them and the real culprits. Isolating the real troublemakers is as a consequence even harder, as policing of this sort creates a siege mentality, where 'England' need to stick together in face of a common, foreign enemy.

Many of the people deported in the way described above were greeted on their arrival back home by newspaper head-lines screaming for tougher action against hooligans, including calls for the banning of anyone suspected – not convicted, just suspected – of hooliganism. It is hardly unreasonable paranoia to suspect that if a government were to begin looking beyond the list of those convicted for candidates to ban, then a list of people deported from a previous tournament could well be an obvious place to start.

There can be different reasons why people aren't convicted. Sometimes it's because bringing guilty people to trial, where evidence is required to convict them, is a lot more complicated than just throwing them out of the country, making them somebody else's problem. Other times it's because they didn't actually do anything wrong.

That's quite a difference, and it's a crucial one. Genuine football fans don't want violent racist thugs in football, and would quite cheerfully see them arrested, prosecuted, convicted and banned from travelling to matches. But we all know that when policing Brussels-style prevails, any one of us could be the people undergoing the nightmares described above. Fans can tell the difference between those who deserve banning and those who are just in the wrong place at the wrong time. It's crucial that the authorities learn to do the same.

Charleroi

Saturday 17th June

GIVEN THE EVENTS of the previous evening and the ensuing press coverage, it was probably inevitable that there would be a somewhat different atmosphere in Charleroi from Eindhoven. Certainly there was an air of expectation among the media, who all had their eyes and cameras trained on the square, watching from all sides.

There are those who say that the presence of a media concentration such as this acts as a catalyst for trouble, as they always seem to be there when it happens. Can't be coincidence, can it? Then again, some people working in the media would have you believe that it is only because of the excellent nose for news that they have developed over years of experience that they happen to be on the spot when trouble starts.

There is an obvious flaw in both arguments. What about the trouble that happens when there is no media presence? No blaming it on the cameras then. Nor can the media 'nose' for trouble be infallible if they miss the story. Perception is important here; maybe the reason why the media always seem to be a factor in trouble is that the only trouble that most people hear about is when the media report it.

It didn't take a genius to work out where large numbers of

English – and German, for that matter – fans would congregate in Charleroi, and any media reporter who didn't check it out would be in line for a bollocking from his or her editor. Nonetheless the sheer weight of numbers of news people there did alter the situation, fuelling the sense of anticipation. And while I wouldn't say that the media were responsible for starting the trouble, they didn't exactly help.

At least the media were responsible for, or played a key part in, two of the more amusing incidents of the day. At one stage there was a bit of a stand-off between the German and English hooligans on either side of the square. First one, then two or three, then more camera crews decided that the best vantage point for filming the two groups as they faced each other would be in the middle between them. The sight of all these camera crews congregating together naturally attracted more attention, until all eyes were focused on the middle of the square and the impressive array of television hardware and personnel on display. The suspense was growing until, all of a sudden – the fountains switched on, sending great plumes of water up into the air and down onto the camera crews, sending them scattering. Oh, how we laughed.

The second one had a smaller audience, but it amused me. As one of our team waited to be interviewed by a Sky News crew, he couldn't help but overhear the telephone conversation one of the producers was having with one of his minions. Conversation might not be quite the right word; he was bellowing instructions. Giving a revealing insight into how their bulletins are put together, he screamed 'No, no, I want *couples!* And when I say give me couples, I want *good looking* couples! Don't send me any more ugly couples!'

Not everything the media did was so amusing, however. In one of the incidents that sparked problems in Charleroi, the media presence was definitely a factor. And before anybody says I'm overplaying this, let's remember that there were in fact only one or two such incidents all day; the large-scale, drawn-out battle of Charleroi everyone talks about never actually happened.

The day was hot, and people were thirsty. So they drank, though admittedly they probably would have drunk if it had been cold and wet too. You got the impression that the Germans were concentrated on the north of the square and the English on the south, but it was only an impression, based on two groups in the centre, either side of the fountains. In fact, wandering around the perimeter you would encounter a complete mixture of English, Germans and locals quite happily sharing bars, even tables.

There were, on both sides, groups of hooligans more than ready for trouble, however, and there was a fair amount of taunting from both sides. The English chanting seemed to focus on World War Two, much of it in very poor taste. There didn't seem to me much point though in remonstrating with them to think about the innocent civilian victims, most of whom never voted for the Nazis, who lost their lives in the flooding caused by the Dam Busters' bouncing bomb. Especially as some of these hooligans probably thought that not voting Nazi was where the innocent civilians had gone wrong.

The Germans were chanting largely in English, and subconsciously it almost felt as though they were making a special effort to make sure their insults were understood. In fact it is a backhanded compliment to the influence of English football fandom that many continental fans chant in English even at home, as a matter of course. They don't seem to realise that while they think it's really cool, to us it sounds a little bit sad.

There wasn't much more to it than tasteless – in both senses

– singing until the police decided to make a move to snatch a couple of German fans from outside a bar. Now I'm not complaining about the arrest itself. For all I know, the two they were nicking could have been guilty of the most heinous crimes of racial hatred and sickening violence, and needed to be taken out. They would presumably have the right to defend themselves in court and prove their innocence if necessary. The arrest itself was fairly efficient; perhaps verging on the ruthlessly rough, but we're all grown-ups, they were clearly targeting people they knew – not a problem.

Where the problem did arise for me was the palaver that accompanied it. I can't prove this, but many of the TV people I spoke to had the same impression – it seemed as though the police had tipped off two or three camera crews, presumably to guarantee quality exposure for their firm and decisive policing. This meant though that rather than just having a streamlined and compact snatch squad of police officers rushing towards their targets, added in to the picture were an extra dozen or so people, complete with TV cameras, sound booms and somebody to point at things. Now there were twenty or so people rushing across the crowded square – and that was just the invitees.

But then there are all the other media people looking on. These are trained professionals. They can sniff out a story from a mile away. So when twenty people including rival camera crews start running in one direction, it's not long before they realise something's happening. Their response is of course to dispatch their own camera, soundman and pointer to the same place. So there are now about forty people charging across the square towards one bar. In a crowded arena like this, with all its beer-soaked combustible material and a simmering atmosphere, a group of forty people running in any one direction has various effects. One is that some people run after them, either out of curiosity or because they assume it's all kicked off. So make that eighty people running. Naturally there are people in the way, so you get them running in different directions. Among the others with entirely innocent intentions, people get bumped into, hard. Drinks get spilt, glasses get broken, tempers get frayed. A table gets knocked over. Before long more furniture is flying through the air.

This is not meant to put the blame for the events in Charleroi on anyone other than the thugs who made their pilgrimage there looking for trouble. All I'm saying is that the media stampede didn't help. It might have been better if the snatch squads just quietly went in, did their job and got out again with the minimum of fuss.

This hostile, edgy atmosphere was, however, largely limited to the square, and though it was crowded, the Place Charles II didn't contain most of the England fans. The bars in the main shopping streets in the lower town, which were nearer to the station, were doing a roaring trade, and it seemed that anyone who was in town for reasons other than the football had climbed the hill. As the trains arrived from Brussels, more and more fans swelled the numbers in and around the pubs and restaurants, where they stayed until maybe an hour before kick off. I watched the look of surprise on the faces of many who on their way to the ground had to pass the square and were astonished to find it cordoned off by a ring of riot police. It may seem completely at odds with the impression at home created by the media reports, but most England fans will have spent the day of the game unaware that there had been any trouble, let alone having been involved in it.

To get things in proportion, it's worth remembering that there were around twenty thousand England fans in town that day, who'd travelled abroad on a mini-holiday and who had made quite a day of it. In that context, the outcome of the day was not nearly as dramatic as it has been portrayed. And while I do not want in any way to belittle or excuse the anti-social behaviour that generated such dramatic television pictures in the square that afternoon, how much lasting damage was actually done?

The water cannon, for instance, were fired from very intimidating looking vehicles. Direct impact from their jets was described as like being kicked by a horse. They made grown men run away. But in the final analysis more than anything else, they made things, er, wet.

And the flying furniture? Throwing chairs and tables around is not nice. It was mostly done with violent intent, and that's reprehensible. Most people, me included, wouldn't argue with furniture throwers being arrested. But let's not lose sight of a couple of things. First the furniture in question was plastic; not by accident, but by arrangement between the local authorities and the bar owners in advance. They did this because plastic furniture would limit the damage.

Second, you have to be the recipient of a direct hit at very close range for a plastic chair to hurt you. This didn't happen very often. Not least because the arseholes throwing them were often too pissed to throw them accurately. Or any distance. And really, there wasn't that much furniture thrown as in many cases those throwing were being severely squirted at the time. And partly as a consequence of being vexed about being squirted, many of the chairs were being thrown at the (armoured) water cannon vehicles. Or more precisely at the concrete pavement in front of the water cannon vehicles, because even though the vehicles were massive and not very far away, most of the throwers missed them. Anybody who hoped that Britain's medal count at the Sydney Olympics could be boosted by the last minute inclusion of the new event of plastic patio furniture throwing had better think again.

The bottom line was that for all the action-packed film footage, not many chairs and tables were thrown, even fewer hit anybody, and most were left intact and back in use for sitting on the next day. I've seen more damage to patio furniture on a windy day at Homebase.

For the couple of five-minute spells when it did kick off, of course, it was very unpleasant. At one point we had to remove the Embassy vehicle from the square as I couldn't guarantee its safety, or more importantly the safety of the volunteers working beside it. I saw England 'fans' for whom the firing of the nearby water cannon was the signal to batter anyone near them they thought deserved it, anyone who brought a beating on themselves by being German or by speaking in a foreign language. I 'rescued' a young German lad, maybe 25 years old, from a kicking by a couple of oafs. It happened immediately in front of me, and I know for a fact that the lad had done absolutely nothing wrong, just walked into the wrong part of the square at the wrong time. The English idiots battering him looked as though they were about to do the same to me when I helped the German lad away, but must have thought better of it, as they just swore at me instead. It's an old cliché, I know, but at that moment I did feel ashamed of being English. I went particularly out of my way to help the German lad to hospital, in the hope that perhaps he might not hold a grudge against every English person for the rest of his life.

There were some unpleasant bastards among the Germans too; it's worth remembering that just about every country in Europe, and beyond, has its own hooligan problem. Also mixed up in the square that day were likely lads from other countries. I bumped into Dutch fan coaches I recognised from the friendly match we played in Eindhoven; they were there to keep an eye on known Dutch hooligans from Utrecht and PSV that had travelled to Belgium. And there were locals, too; a far right-influenced group of Charleroi fans who called themselves the 'Walloon Boys' and who were notorious throughout – well, throughout parts of Charleroi, at least.

One small point in passing: sadly I can't go along with the very neat idea that people who get involved in hooliganism of this nature 'aren't football fans', a notion often expressed by press commentators. I fully understand and sympathise with the sentiment behind this saying, and I wish it were true. And it is, in the narrow sense that they clearly don't have the good of the game at heart. But the idea that they don't understand or know about football is not true. It's just not that simple. Some of these people who blight football do actually know a lot about it, and care passionately about how their team – club or country – performs. They don't see any contradiction between their behaviour and their love of football. I do, but they don't. Often in quick media interviews I'd try to draw a distinction between 'genuine football fans' and hooligans, in order to emphasis the fact that not all, in fact proportionately very few, England fans cause any trouble. In reality though, I'm well aware that the distinctions are much more complex, and that are a lot of shades of grey. Some of the worst thugs know quite a lot about football. In fact it wouldn't surprise me if they funded their trips to Euro 2000 with their winnings from football pub quizzes. Bastards.

Anyway, two or three bursts of clumsy and drunkenly inefficient violence, each two or three minutes long, gave the world the TV pictures they'd been expecting and provided a justification for some heavy policing of the town centre. And of the railway station too, where trainloads of incoming fans were stopped and searched by police, scores being arrested for not being able to produce their passport, even if they did have a match ticket. Arriving with a passport but without a match ticket was also for some not enough, and they were either arrested or sent back to Brussels on the next train. Some fans told me that their mates had been advised by policemen on the station platform to leave their money and passports in left luggage lockers in the station, and had then been arrested immediately on leaving the building for not having their money and passports with them.

But despite all of this, most England fans who were in Charleroi that day will tell you that it was a great occasion, historic and unforgettable. And though I'd put in a long day, I got a second wind late in the afternoon as the adrenaline began to kick in. I had a match ticket.

I'd had plenty of experience for one lifetime of being not far away when historic England games took place. Being nearby is not quite the same as being there though, and for once I was lucky, or as others might see it, devious. Devious, in that I deliberately hadn't joined in too strenuously in the clamour for a Portugal ticket in the knowledge that I'd have a moral edge in the argument over which of our team got into the Germany game.

There was an excitement and tension you could touch on the way up to the stadium before the match. I'd forgotten to eat earlier in the day – or if I had eaten, I'd forgotten about it now – and I was starving. So we called into a burger bar which could lay justifiable claim to the slowest service of 'fast' food anywhere in Europe. There were queues out of the door, but the staff at the counter were completely unruffled as they stuck to their tried and tested system. Every customer got individual attention. So individual, that they would take one person's order, then cook his or her food and serve it to them before taking the next person's order. People who dared to suggest that they could perhaps take several orders at once, cook a few burgers simultaneously and thereby speed up the service were met with a withering look that suggested that they needed to understand that that wasn't the way they did things around here. In the circumstances the patience of the England fans in the queue was admirable, though it was probably just as well that the staff didn't slow the process down any further by asking customers to fill in a 'comments and suggestions' customer feedback form while they waited. I couldn't help but be amused when, on looking back at the restaurant exterior as I walked up the hill towards the stadium, I spotted its name. 'Quick'.

There was a good-natured squash at the first cordon, and again at the second. The entrance into the England stand itself was a lot less pleasant. The stadium does not have turnstiles, and there was a big and eager crowd having to pass through a very narrow space. Once through, there came the body searches, so even when the gateway had been penetrated there was no room for the welcome relief of spilling forward. The crush outside was positively dangerous; I was struck by the irony of all the fuss over the rake of the stands when this entirely foreseeable problem had gone unremarked.

Eventually I got in and found my seat, well placed behind the goal. The ground looked great, bathed in sunshine, and the atmosphere pre-match was superb. A hint of nervous anticipation certainly, yet mixed with a feeling of confidence that history didn't really justify.

The match itself wasn't really a classic, but that doesn't really matter, does it? England won, because Shearer scored.

God, I enjoyed that goal. I was not exactly alone in that, of course. But among all the generalised euphoria that engulfed the red-shirted hordes as his header hit the net, I felt a special pride. Even at that climactic moment of ecstasy I'd allowed myself a fleeting moment of indulgence, inwardly and invisibly sneering my smug contempt at the thousands of converts to the wonder of Shearer. These same people would not have hesitated a few short weeks ago to give him all sorts of grief as he visited their grounds, or to have denounced him as finished, yesterday's man, over a pre-match pint. They've changed their tune now. Now they're all joining in with the chant of 'Shearer, Shearer!'

The negativity didn't last long. Drawing on vague recollections from a long-gone Presbyterian past of some biblical reference that there is more rejoicing in heaven at the repentance of one sinner than at ten righteous men, or something, I forgave them all their trespasses and clutched them to my bosom. Metaphorically. Because this was historic. England had beaten the Germans.

Well, it certainly felt historic at the time. The benefit of hindsight might put things in a slightly different light. This was after all a one-goal victory, ground out against what general consensus held to be the worst German side to turn out in a major tournament for at least a generation. Plus the fact that the Germans probably had the better of the first half. And, looking back, it was England's only victory before the early exit, out before the knockout rounds even began. Let's face it, the somewhat dodgy song popular among sections of England's support is not dramatically improved by reference to it: 'Two World Wars, one World Cup and one European Championships game (group stage)'? Doesn't even scan.

It was certainly historic though in the sense that a lot had happened since the last time. The 1966 final seems very familiar to everybody, even though most match-going fans these days probably have no personal recollection of it. I was six at the time, and living in the town of Ashington, Northumberland, which as well as being my birthplace had also given the world the Charlton brothers. Hardly surprising then that there was a bit of a fuss there around that time. But in all honesty, my clear impression of the sequence of events during the game itself has all been formed since then, from re-runs of the game topped up with regular reminders on quiz shows.

Just think about all the dim, distant, almost forgotten events that have happened since 1966. The moon landing. Decimal currency. The Scaffold at Number One with 'Lily the Pink'. West Bromwich Albion winning the cup. That's all a long time ago.

(Yes, yes, I know. Cheap shot at West Brom. And you have to go back another 11 years to find Newcastle's last FA Cup success. I'm well aware of all that. But a cheap shot's a cheap shot.)

And it is more than just the length of time, it's also the games in between, and the way they were lost. The following World Cup in Mexico it was in the quarter-final. Then twice in semi-finals, in the 1990 World Cup in Italy, and at home in Euro '96. Even worse, both semis were lost on penalties. It's no wonder this meant a lot.

I must confess to having quite liked the German team in the past. Being an awkward and cantankerous character by nature, I've made a point of winding up my mates by betting on the Germans in big tournaments. They've won me quite a bit of money over the years, bless them, more than they objectively should have done, probably because anti-German prejudice has an effect in restricting the amount of money the bookies take on them, thereby keeping the odds long.

The Germans have often had good, efficient teams that conform to all their national stereotypes, rather than the flair and style which has won admiration for the Brazilians, the

Dutch, sometimes the Italians and more recently the French. This summer they had neither style nor efficiency, and they went home without a victory, tails between their legs. And they didn't half take some stick for it.

Thanks to their defeat in Charleroi, the deriding of the national team by the media began a good four days earlier in Germany than it did in England. One after another, former players and coaches queued up to slate their country's performance. Gunter Netzer, European Championship winner in 1980: 'The team never had a chance of putting the English in difficulty.' Thomas Helmer, medal winner in Euro '96: 'I've got a feeling things aren't 100% right with the team, or with the manager.' Helmut Haller, who scored Germany's opening goal back in the 1966 final: 'With the football we're playing at the minute, we'll never score.' Paul Breitner, World Cup winner in 1974: 'Whatever happened to the confidence that marked out the German teams of the last 35 years, that brought us so many successes and triumphs?' Not to be left out, current team members joined in. Jens Jeremies: 'You could see that at international level we're just not good enough. It's nothing to do with bad luck. The state of the national team is deplorable.' And goalkeeper Oliver Kahn: 'We don't have the quality, we don't have the players. We can't look to the future with any confidence.'

Cheery souls. Five days later, the German Government Minister for Sport capped them all with a classic Freudian slip, referring to the German players in an interview as 'the ladies'.

There was hardly a German to be seen in the town centre after the game, most of them heading straight down the motorway for home. Most of the England fans had some distance to cover to get to bed that night too, but somehow it didn't seem to matter. There was celebrating to be done, and in the absence of many bars still open, the obvious place to congregate was the fountains. Not beside them, of course, but in them.

What is it with football fans and fountains? There seems to be some deeply ingrained connection between the celebration of a football victory and running water, for fans of all nations. But if there's such a thing as a nation whose fans have a special allegiance to fountains, it must be the Scots again.

I don't know where this comes from, maybe it's a throwback to the seductive sound of Highland streams, but there's something about fountains that Scots football fans seem to find irresistible. Of course every nation's fans, probably even every club's fans, have among their number devotees of cascading water in an incongruous urban setting, but no one seems to take to it in the same numbers, with the same relish as the Scots. There's not a waterfall outside a Hotel de Ville anywhere in the world too cold for a Scotsman to kneel under, nor a statue of a saint or war hero that doesn't look better with orange hair and tartan bunnet. The architectural beauty of great cities like Paris or Rome or Amsterdam, with their rich culture, steeped in history, can be appreciated much more deeply if you're soaking wet at the time. Unless of course it's raining, but that's a different sort of wet. With fountains, you decide you want to get wet. And being in a fountain is a way of sharing your joy, everyone can see you must be having a really good time. And while it's a special experience for each individual, it's also a collective pleasure, when all your mates from your 'scheme' are there in that same continental fountain with you.

If there's something special about Scotsmen and fountains, it's manifested most clearly in the kilts. Kilts and fountains were clearly made for each other. That's not to suggest that all kilts respond to fountains in the same way. Again drawing on personal observation, there seems to be two distinct ways a kilt can react to fountains, or more accurately to the pool of water at the base of the fountain. It should be noted that no matter how deep the water is, it always comes up to a Scotsman's waist. This has more to do with the Scotsman than anything else. Some lucky ones find fountains with waist-deep pools around them – that's the easy way. Others have to kneel down, making it that much easier for the water to reach their waist level. Sadly, it is a current trend, in these days of environmental awareness and water conservation, for fountains more and more often to be surrounded by glorified puddles of water only a few inches deep. This however only means that the Scotsman has to engage in ever-greater contortions to get the water up to his waist. It nearly always can and will be done.

Roughly half of the kilts I had observed in Parisian fountains back in June 1998 floated. That is, they lay spread out on the surface of the water, radiating out from the Scotsman's waist, creating an effect like a giant jellyfish with a Tam O'Shanter, a sort of Scottish Man o' War. This is visually very appealing, although it does raise issues of decency in some cases. It's just as well that very few fountains in central Paris are tidal.

The other half of the kilts monitored didn't float, but hung down by the Scotsman's legs, under the water. This may be connected to the level of absorbency of the material, but I have another theory. I think it may be to do with shyness or modesty. I reckon many Scotsmen, knowing that they're going to a match abroad and are therefore inevitably going to end up in a fountain wearing a kilt, hire the said garment a few days early. This allows time for their mother to sew fishing weights into the hem, thereby preserving their decency and making it less likely they'll be arrested or frighten children.

In Charleroi, funnily enough, there weren't many kilts in

sight, either weighted or floating. There were however plenty of people cavorting under fountains. Apart from those who'd come by car and had parked to the north of the city, or who were staying locally, the England fans virtually all had to pass through or by the square on their way to get their trains. So nearly everybody had the chance for a quick dip before they boarded their trains. It must have seemed a good idea at the time, and it certainly provided much more positive television images. But speaking as one who has yet to enjoy the fountain experience, I've always suspected that three-quarters-of-an-hour later, when you're sitting on an unheated late-night train and squelching obscenely every time you move, perhaps it may all feel very different.

Everybody was far too happy, triumphant, to initiate any repeat of the events of the afternoon. Though the riot police were out in force, by and large all that they had to do was to wait for the crowds to disperse and make their way home, or at least elsewhere.

Later I learned that not everything had been quite so straightforward in the town centre during the game itself. There had been a lot of fans without tickets and as ever most of them were watching the game, without any problems, cheerfully and noisily in bars. But there had been a few who'd tried, unsuccessfully, to storm their way into the ground by trying to pull down the fences, and there had been problems in one or two bars in town. I also heard stories of English fans fighting among themselves, club against club, though most of the people who told me about it said that it hadn't really amounted to much.

As ever in these circumstances, it seemed that a small minority had been involved, but they'd succeeded in making life unpleasant for ordinary, innocent fans as a result of the police response. Some of the stories we were told later made familiarly depressing and depressingly familiar reading.

Martin Carruthers travelled to Charleroi with a friend, having bought tickets back home for the game against Romania. They arrived in Charleroi on the Saturday, and watched the Germany game in a cafe not far from the station.

My friend and I left the cafe around the 80 minute mark as we were meeting our two other friends who had tickets for the game, to get a lift to a camp site that we had obtained details of earlier. As we walked outside we were told in no uncertain terms by the police that we were arrested and that everybody in the cafe would be detained. If we came now with no trouble, they would co-operate with us; if not, force would be used.

During a conversation with somebody else later in the cell I learned that they were told we would be kept for about two hours.

We were then searched and stripped of our possessions, passport and all. We were handcuffed with white plastic strips which dug in and bruised the skin, and made to sit outside a shop, individual numbers stickered to our arms.

After 60 minutes or so we were led slowly down a number of side streets before once again being ordered to sit. Some, but very little may I add, water was passed around and they would only loosen a few strips that were digging in — the police by this time had removed their helmets and were messing about with one another.

We were then herded onto a bus and travelled for about

30 minutes, once up to a courtyard but for some reason back out again before returning slowly. We were then kept on this bus for up to two hours, and only in the last 30 minutes did they let people use the toilet and have again what little water was available.

We were led off the bus and placed into our first cell – approximately 60 fans in the cell. Our possessions were kept outside. There was one toilet, no water and no blankets – it was now about one or two in the morning and with wearing only shorts and T-shirt from the day it was quite cold!

We were then led out to sign a form. The person leading me spoke little English, and in the broken English they did have said it was a form declaring that our possessions were being kept for a while. We were then led to drop off our possessions at an office. At this point one fan was talking to his officer and asked what was on the form – his said assault – so I asked if he would read mine. It said 'causing a disruption outside the cafe' – as I have said, we walked out and co-operated with the police! I told the policeman this and he apologised half-heartedly.

We were then led to our second cell. Again there was no water or blankets, and it was very cold. We were kept here for about two hours, it was now about six or seven in the morning. There were only about 30 to 50 fans this time – they had been calling us out one by one from about five o'clock onwards – and I was released at around ten past seven.

Another fan, who described himself as *Prisoner RG026*-13 told us:

My three friends and I had joined a large group of England fans to watch the match in one of, seemingly, only two bars in Charleroi that was showing the football. Shortly before half-time I noticed a disturbance outside caused by two groups of rival English club (Notts County and Derby) 'supporters'. The trouble continued for about ten minutes before both groups of supporters ran inside the bar to escape from the Belgian police that had just arrived on the scene. I would estimate that maybe only 10% of the people trapped in that bar had been involved in the trouble. My friends and I decided to abandon the viewing of the match in order to attempt to make our way back to our car and the ferry back to England. When we approached the police and explained that we wanted to leave Charleroi peacefully to return to England we were told that we had two options: 'Voluntary arrest', or 'Violence, then arrest'. We took the first option.

Up until our 'processing' and subsequent ten hour detention in a holding cell we can have no complaint about the attitude of the Belgian police (barring the decision to handcuff two of my friends tightly behind their back).

However, upon being locked in the holding pen things became substantially worse. There was no differentiation made between the voluntary and non-voluntary arrests and the police would not answer any questions about our civil rights or possible deportations. The cells themselves were abysmal. 70, mostly innocent people, locked in an open-air cell for ten hours. We were promised and then denied any form of bedding or blankets. One urinal was provided for all to use and only a small percentage of those arrested were offered food (a small cold waffle), and 'bags' of water were provided to share between us. The cell floor itself was wet and too cold to either sit or lay on. Those who did attempt to sleep awoke, freezing and shivering from their *cold concrete mattress. Most of us stood or walked around for the duration of our ten hour stay. We were arrested at 10pm on the Saturday and released without charge at 8am the following day. No explanation or apology was made and we were ordered to leave. We left.*

The subsequent vilification of England supporters by the Belgian authorities and UEFA has left all of us sick and angry – especially in light of the attitude taken towards other countries hooligan element, especially the well organised and vicious Turkish hooligan element.

His story is corroborated by another fan, who offered an explanation for the wet cell floors:

We were in a bar when we heard, then saw, a lot of people running about in the street outside. We didn't see any actual trouble, but assumed there must have been a problem. The police said that if we didn't all come out of the bar voluntarily we would be tear-gassed and beaten up, so my friend and I came straight out, thinking this to be the sensible option. We were voluntarily arrested, and then loads more people came out of the bar and were allowed to go!

We were thrown in the back of a van, then put in a cell with about 80 others, in the freezing cold. When we asked for blankets they filled the cell with water and said 'now you have to stand up'. I was detained until the next morning.

Brussels

Saturday 17th June

EVENTS AFTER THE game, as fans arrived back in Brussels by train, happened too late to make the Sunday papers. Events in Brussels all day happened too far away for me to be able to give anything like an eye-witness account. The Embassy did have a team of volunteers in Brussels that day though, as part of our commitment to be, within the obvious limitations, where England's fans are. Leading our team in the capital that day was Alison Pilling, who up until a fortnight earlier had been the national chair of the FSA, and was now its treasurer. (In other words, she was paying my wages, which might explain the polite, even deferential, terms in which I refer to her.) Anyway, it is an honour and a privilege to allow her to relate the story of match day in Brussels, maintaining the first-hand nature of this book. Take it away, Alison!

We headed for Brussels Midi station on Saturday afternoon, all five of us wearing our official Fans Embassy t-shirts. We put piles of FSA fanzines on stands intended for train timetables, unattended help desks for various sponsors, and on the counter of any place selling alcohol (targeting your clientele effectively is an important part of the process, you see). Actually it was quite a challenge for my schoolgirl French to explain what it was all about. It is in situations like this that I have found a friendly smile is worth a thousand words, those words going something like: 'I know you don't know what this magazine is. It may, who knows, contain an Editorial inciting the English to violence; it may be a political treatise on the corrupt nature of the Belgian State; it may explain the true way to live your life by someone with a name more bizarre than L. Ron Hubbard. All this is as nothing when you are asked to put it on the bar by a simpering lass with the eager-to-please look usually associated with those doe-eyed squirrels from Disney cartoon movies.' Anyway, I found it a most effective strategy, so don't knock it.

We also gave out fanzines to supporters coming off the Eurostar and others we met around the Station. That was when we met Jamie and his mates who had been in Brussels a little over two hours. This was their experience of Euro 2000 so far:

> As soon as we arrived in Brussels, we went for a couple of drinks and a bit of singing in a bar with some other England lads. We then decided to get a taxi to the station and make our way to Charleroi. We were having a great time, singing songs in the taxi and cracking jokes with the driver. We stopped at a junction and then someone came out of a nearby bar, leaned in the car window and sprayed a canister of Mace all around the inside of the taxi. The driver was great, but he couldn't believe what had happened and struggled to drive with tears streaming down his face. All of us were having trouble breathing. I am sure they did it to us because we were English.

When we met the lads, their eyes were still red and swollen 40 minutes later, and they were angry. They said they had been attacked by a Turk and when I asked if they were sure, they replied – quite reasonably – that they 'didn't have time to ask him for his fucking passport.'

I don't know how to respond to English fans with these kind of experiences, who have no quarrel with anyone, but feel forced to take sides in an argument they didn't start.

By and large, however, our experience of giving out fanzines was brilliant. Around the bars at one end of the Grande Place, hundreds of England fans were drinking and chatting in the blazing sunshine. The atmosphere was positive and relaxed with everyone looking forward to the match against the Germans. I certainly didn't hear any choruses of the racist songs that appeared common currency in some other places. The only note of tension was when we asked people about their experiences on Friday night. The story was the same everywhere – that England fans were reviled as hooligans but no one seemed to want to hear about the threats and abuse from locals wielding frightening weapons; or about the fans who were too terrified to leave their hotel rooms for 24 hours. Sitting in a bar a few days later, one lad said to me, 'Who speaks for us? Who speaks for England fans?'

The FSA tries to play that role as well as we are able, and if people are bored with or sceptical of the constant repetition of the experiences of the 'vast majority of ordinary, decent fans', it's because there is no other established means of those opinions being expressed.

Anyway, Brussels was great. The weather was glorious, the beer cold and Belgian, lots of happy, expectant people. One gang of lads we met had all dressed in Richard The Lionheart crusader gear. Not that Richard the First is much of a role model but it was done as a good laugh. I'm pretty certain that their choice of daywear didn't reflect a desire to sack foreign cities and chase off the infidel.

Racism was, however, a problem at the Central Railway

Station. Platform Four was crammed with perhaps three hundred England fans singing and chanting as they waited for the Charleroi train (and we handed out more bloody fanzines). It was all good-humoured with everyone joining in, with the exception of the long line of police lazing against the barrier overlooking the main hall out of sight of the platform, although not out of earshot. There was a small group of around 20 men who were leading the songs, beginning with that old favourite 'Ingerland, Ingerland, Ingerland', the station ringing with the sound. The second song in their repertoire was 'No Surrender', at which point about half the people stopped singing, and although the platform was about as full as it could be, a space began to form around the group. With the third song, the now notorious 'I'd rather be a Paki than a Turk', they were the only people still singing, but as a very vocal minority they'd set their stamp on the rest of us. The only way we had been able to object was to shut up.

By late afternoon, our fanzine work was nearly done and we had to consider the difficult task of getting a good view of the match, given the limited number of decent-sized television sites in the area. The previous night, however, we had found a decent place boasting good food and the largest TV set possible before it could go around calling itself a giant screen, located on the quaintly named Street of the Cretinous Man. Being a restaurant, however, meant that in order to watch both Romania/Portugal and England/Germany we would have to make the meal last close on four hours. Given how efficient the service was, this could mean perhaps seven or eight courses so a different approach was called for. We managed to see most of the first match by getting couple of rounds in, as an 'aperitif' you understand, before telling them that we weren't hungry yet and could we come back in a little while. Hard negotiations resulted in their promising us a table but not necessarily the choice one we were now occupying. Returning 10 or 15 minutes before kick-off, we were allocated a table side-on to the TV, but without the restricted view pillar that had marred Jim's £70 match-going experience. The only obstructions were a couple of noisy Danes and a large, lone Englishman, who looked as though he was already several courses through his eight-course meal, an opinion reinforced by his comfy chair pitch-side.

The first 20 minutes of the match passed calmly (order taken, slow and measured consumption of garlic bread), although we had a scare on 27 minutes with the arrival of the main course. It was around this time that I got the first of several calls from Jamal.

I should explain that the distinctive feature of any Fans Embassy volunteer is not only the white shirt, but also a pathological over-reliance on the mobile phone. I cannot imagine how anyone ever managed to keep track of a team of 15 or 20 people without them, and can only assume that in those heady pre-mobile days of the Italia '90 Fans Embassy, the team developed a peculiar form of telepathy. The downside, of course, to greater communication with your team-mates, is enforced communication with all sorts of people that you don't want to talk to. Not that I didn't want to talk to Jamal, but well into the first half of England-Germany at 0–0 wasn't my most communicative time. Jamal was a Belgian Fan Coach – effectively a youth worker who was working with local young people around the football. I'd also had chats with Moussa, a French Fan Coach from Marseille, and with Willem, Belgian again. I hadn't actually met any of these people. However, Jamal rang to say that he was on the Grande Place and could we meet, so I told him where we were sitting and turned back to the match, giving the Large Lone Englishman an encouraging smile.

Jamal was adamant that we should meet other Fan Coaches,

including those working with Turkish fans and with the local 'Prevention Officer'. It seemed lost on these people that there was a match going on but Jamal said the meeting place was just around the corner so I said that I'd come round at half-time for a few minutes.

At 9.33pm I was standing at the appointed place, looking nervously between my watch and the empty street. It was a full three or four minutes later that the other fan workers turned up, mostly lads but one noticeable woman who would not have looked out of place in an old Shabba Ranks video – you know the look, black cycling shorts, Wonderbra and pouting lips and a name like Paulette or Michaela.

So by 9.41pm (with only five or six minutes to second-half kick-off), we settled down in a back room in the local police station where we were about to be introduced to Ilse, the local Prevention Officer. Jamal had explained that she was independent of the police, although I can't help thinking that meeting in a police station didn't exactly reinforce her independence. She had in front of her, not one, not two, but three mobile phones, and as noted they always ring when you least want them to. So it was that I spent the first two minutes of the second-half watching Ilse answer her phones. It did eventually cross her mind that chairing a meeting and answering the phones were mutually exclusive and turned them off. We introduced ourselves, the others in the room being fan workers from Holland, Belgium, France, Turkey and Denmark, I think. Ilse began, in French, to recount events of the previous night. Now I've said my French isn't great, but roughly translated it went something like: 'Brussels was a nightmare last night because England fans were rioting all over the place and the police couldn't control it.' She eventually stopped and spoke to me in English, begging me to 'control my people'. It was tempting to slam my fist on the table and bellow Moses-like 'let my people go', but I'm pretty certain that the 40,000 or so people following England that day didn't really feel they belonged to me. Anyway I explained that the best way to lessen problems was to protect England fans from attack by local people and to arrest only those who were actually causing problems, not bar-loads of people regardless of anything as complex as evidence. She seemed particularly defensive and argued that the police had had so many problems that indiscriminate arrest was inevitable. The significance of her independence was becoming increasingly lost on me.

During this exchange a man entered the room (9.55pm, at the same moment as Phil Neville passed a sweet left-footer down the line – if that doesn't prove I missed the match, what will?). I got the impression that he was some kind of top policeman, and he seemed sympathetic to what I was saying. It became clear that the police's main concern was that youths from the local communities would turn out onto the streets armed, if the police couldn't guarantee their people's safety. All this had been heightened by the assault of a young local North African woman the night before, her attackers allegedly English. Simply put, the police were a lot more worried by the prospect of thousands of angry local youths on the streets than they were by the approbation of a few England fans.

At this point (9.58pm), my phone rang and Paul shouted 'what a goal!' 'Have we scored?' I asked in the sort of voice that I hoped conveyed my excitement but also how pissed off I was not to be witnessing anything. I turned back to Ilse and explained that her problems were over – England were winning. She looked at me blankly. 'England,' I explained, 'are playing a football match tonight. We are winning.' She still looked blank but I couldn't think of anything to say other than to go back to first principles and explain that her country – Belgium – was, as we spoke, hosting a large football competition.

Ilse then went on to say her information was that a fight had been arranged for 10.30pm at the Bourse. I expressed my doubts about the time, as I hadn't seen many England fans around, most being in Charleroi either in the stadium or in the bars round about, but I agreed that The Bourse was a likely flashpoint (time now 10.02pm). The Bourse is ordinarily just a nice enough building but its significance is that it lies on the main road that forms the boundary between touristy Brussels with its bars, restaurants and kitsch shops, and the bit of Brussels that real people live in – in this case its North African and Turkish communities. So I agreed that we would go there after the match to observe.

As the meeting broke up, Paulette leaned over to me and said, "These English men, why do they do it? They are economically deprived, yes? Perhaps they have no self-esteem. This is why they are hooligans." 10.04pm – time to go.

Back at the restaurant, my place (and my dessert) had been saved for me, but I was much too annoyed to push through the crowds now standing round the TV to sit down. As we counted down the last few minutes, Large Lone Englishman was getting increasingly agitated and noisy chanting was coming from the bar next door. We were beginning to believe we might actually beat the Germans. It was strange watching the match standing alongside tourists of other nations merely watching a not terribly inspiring performance from two nations that used to be able to play a bit. With the final whistle, LLE broke down and wept, to the dismay of other diners, so I went over and gave him a hug so he knew he wasn't alone. And after all, he was one of 'my people' even if I couldn't vouch for his being 'under control' for the rest of the evening.

We flashed our 'Official Euro 2000 Fan Co-ordinator' cards at the police cordon around the Grande Place, as merely saying 'good-humoured England fans coming through' had had little impact. The Place was almost entirely filled with tourists who appeared oblivious to our glorious victory. I say almost entirely. One person was busy giving them a clue.

The Grande Place is over a hundred yards long, and nearly as wide, so if you ran all the way round, you'd probably need to catch your breath at the end. If you ran round it twice, however, with both arms outstretched holding a full plastic beer glass in one hand, whilst singing *The Dam Busters* theme tune, without hesitation, deviation or repetition, not only would you be out of breath but you would have made a complete tit of yourself in front of a couple of thousand people. But you had to appreciate the sentiment, so when we passed a prone body a few seconds later, whooping noisily as he tried to extract every last bit of oxygen from the air around him, we shook him by the hand.

There was another giant screen TV outside a bar next to The Bourse where a couple of hundred people had been watching the match. As we approached, the bar was closing, presumably on police advice. Groups of England, and Germany fans, as well as fans of other nations, including Turkey, and local lads, ambled peaceably away. We strolled around the streets but were unable to find a fight anywhere, despite Ilse's 'information'. So we decided to go up to Central Station to find out when the trains from Charleroi were coming in. The station was deserted except for 20 or 30 policemen so we chatted to the one who looked in charge and whose English was pretty good. He told us when trains were due and how many people would be on them, totalling around six thousand. None were due until after midnight so we had no choice but to drink beer for an hour.

On our return the information had changed, with our tame policeman explaining that no trains were now stopping at Central Station on the orders of the mayor. All would now stop at the South Station (Midi), so we studied a map of Brussels. If you were one of those six thousand England fans and your train stopped a mile or two down the road from your hotel in central Brussels, which route would you take back? There is only one major road, the one that passes The Bourse. Now at the risk of labouring the point, could this be the same Bourse that ninety minutes earlier the police had said was potentially a major flashpoint? Yes, it was. Could it be that this bizarre change in transport policy would bring the bulk of England fans through the communities whom police had said were ready to arm themselves if there were problems? Yes, again. We decided to try to meet England fans before they reached The Bourse at least to witness how the police had handled things. Well, we would have done had there been any police at that point to witness. To be fair, there were a couple of police vans parked up near The Bourse, but the arrival of England fans seemed the signal for them to leave. Not that there were any obvious problems and everyone was chatting happily about the match, if a little subdued if you consider what the result had been.

We later heard that quite a few people had been beaten up or robbed at knifepoint in the dark streets around Midi station. A larger number had not seen the match at all as they had been arrested for its duration largely through not carrying their passport and then released without charge on the final whistle – not a policy guaranteed to spread goodwill and it accounted for at least one person telling us that they'd followed England for 30 years but this time they'd had more than they could take.

Not so, England fan, John Pude, whose experience of the day had been pretty good:

I travelled to Brussels and carried out all recommendations enclosed in the comprehensive and informative literature sent to me from the England Members' Club. On arrival in Brussels, I was informed of high levels of trouble in Charleroi, and made a decision to travel to the game as soon as possible, so as to maximise the likelihood of early and safe entry to the ground. I arranged to meet some friends in Brussels after the game. I arrived at the stadium approximately two hours before kick-off, and had an unhindered entrance to the ground, although I did have my possessions scrutinised, in good order and patience I felt confident that the authorities were doing a professional job. The atmosphere built, and as we all know, we won. Excellent.

On leaving the ground I returned to the train station to travel to Brussels. There was a minor communication problem with security staff regarding the destination of the trains at Charleroi, but eventually got on one of the Brussels bound trains. The train was full, but not overcrowded, and the train departed on time.

Up until this point everything seemed to be running smoothly.

We were 'deposited' in Brussels at the South station, and advised to walk back to Brussels Central. Although the police presence was high there, it reassured me, as I was travelling alone, to know they were there. I arrived at the bar near the Central station as was pre-arranged at around 1am, as I had become lost, but managed to gather my bearings by use of clear and concise directions from various Police officers on my route.

I purchased a beer, and sat on the pavement tables, enjoying a balmy evening and awaiting my friends' return.

Meanwhile on my way to the Bourse I was receiving regular information from Willem by phone about trouble spots. The most bizarre of these calls was when we reached the Bourse itself, a scene of complete calm, with bars gradually closing, MacDonald's still churning out burgers and everyone making their slow way back to bars and hotels.

'We are withdrawing, Alison,' said Willem, a little intimate considering we still hadn't met. 'There is a riot at the Bourse, it is too dangerous to stay there.' I looked around checking behind pillars and any other hidden corners.

'Where?' I asked. 'I can't find it.' Willem, somewhat perplexed, asked me where I was and went back to check his source. And that, I hoped, was that.

We continued watching as fans walked past us and up through the narrow streets mostly on our side of the road. Three or four fans, all wearing red England tops, were wandering along the other side of the road, however, and this appeared to be the signal for a group of perhaps eight local teenagers to throw bottles and sticks at them. The England lads immediately ran across the road, showers of stones following them, and came directly towards, well . . . towards us actually. We ducked behind an advertising hoarding just in time to avoid being the first casualties of the night.

The whole incident lasted around 20 seconds with two or three hundred England fans near enough to witness what had happened. Most just got out of the way but about 12 or 15 lads appeared to give chase. Since they weren't wearing colours, I couldn't swear they were 'ours' but it seemed likely. They stopped long enough to trash a car on their way past and then ran off down the opposite streets in pursuit.

Now up to this point I was pretty clear about what I'd witnessed but what was happening became increasingly less obvious. The absence of police up to this point was completely without explanation to me and I felt very strongly that they had to take a lot of responsibility for anything that followed from this incident. It was only now that police vans drew up on the main road about a hundred yards to either side of us, but it was unclear about what they were trying to do.

In a quiet moment, I managed to ring one of the Radio Five Live reporters we knew. He said there were incidents further up the road where England fans were a large part of the problem, but we weren't able to get close enough to see. They later told us that they owed their bravery to their wearing 'stab jackets'. Until that point I had assumed their bulging midriffs reflected over-indulgence in chips, beer and mayonnaise.

In another part of town, John had also met the police.

A small van containing police was parked opposite the bar, but they seemed no more interested in the patrons of the bar, than we were of them. After a period of maybe 20 minutes, the police donned helmets and shields and surrounded the bar. At first I thought they were 'protecting' the bar, as there were no problems with anyone inside or outside the establishment. I finished my drink, and went to buy another. No sooner had I done this, than a mass rush into the bar was followed by genuine fear, the like of which I have never experienced, and hope never to do so as long as I live.

The police had fired some kind of gas canister into the small restaurant and the only option to everyone was to leave. Once outside I was confronted with gas mask equipped officers screaming at me to sit down immediately. The floor was covered in puddles of beer, as well as the remains of the plastic pint pots from the outside tables. I did as ordered, and was instantly surprised by the volume and intensity of officials surrounding me and fellow patrons, who totalled only around 50.

I was instructed by a young, uniformed officer to place my hands behind my back in order to be handcuffed with large plastic cable ties. I complied, and was lifted into a line of 30 randomly selected individuals who had also been immobilised in this way. We were helped, roughly though not aggressively to our feet one at a time. We were then marched through the police line and onto a waiting police bus, watched by several photographers and film crews. I was genuinely scared of what would happen to me. Unfortunately these fears were well founded.

We were driven for around 20 minutes, arriving at a 'prison' type building, only to be held for a further hour on the bus, without any fresh air or toilet facilities.

Throughout this period, I was genuinely impressed by the positive of the fans on the bus. It was decided that we may be part of a 'filtering' system, and would be released once all our documentation had been scrutinised, as trouble with officers unable to speak English made for hard information gathering.

I was the first to be removed, and I informed the desk officer of my medical condition and requested the use of a phone to contact the British consulate, as advised in my supporters' pack. This request was flatly denied, and I was uncuffed, and ordered to complete a form with my name and address. My papers, including England Members club card, stub from England vs. Germany ticket, passport, rail pass, apartment address and credit card were inspected. As I have no convictions and was in possession of these details, I was hopeful that I would be 'processed' quickly and be able to meet with my friends.

I was frisked, and had a photo taken. I then had my laces removed from my training shoes and was placed in a cell. The cell was a grey box, around 20 feet by 40 feet. All windows and doors had been bricked up, water and rotting food were on the floor and a small urinal was in the corner. There were five other detainees, whom, they informed me had been there for over 24 hours. I was very worried. For around one hour the cell filled with the men from the bus, yet no further blankets or supplies were placed in the cell.

For the next 12 hours, our cell, now containing 35 men,

was furnished with 15 more blankets, of which many were damp, having possibly been washed but not dried. One box of sweet waffles, and a good quantity of water, supplied in plastic bags, were also handed in. The bags, though, frequently spilled, causing the floor to become even wetter.

With the only ventilation being provided by a wire door at one end, the conditions rapidly deteriorated. Not being allowed to wash, or change clothes, our gas soaked clothes, and lack of personal hygiene made the air stagnant and unpleasant.

At the Bourse, we were not feeling at all safe and in such situations, there is a tendency to follow the herd instinct – the only problem being whose herd? We walked towards one cavalcade of police vans keeping close to the shop fronts to look inconspicuous and in amongst other England fans. We soon realised, however, that these were the wrong sort of England fans, as quite a few were trying to round up their fellow fans to 'get the Turks'. We stepped back from the main road as we'd seen the police's attitude to those 'in the wrong place at the wrong time'. Half a minute later, we found ourselves in amongst quite a different crowd. Small groups of young men, most probably North African, were walking around in a manner that most definitely suggested vigilantism. Some had large dogs, one a Rottweiler, on heavy leashes; some carried strong metal chains or large wooden clubs; and all wore large jackets that might conceal other weapons. We decided not to speak for a while, as spoken English might be the signal these men were waiting for.

Further up the road, as we staged a tactical withdrawal, about 30 men walked in the opposite direction, all wearing dark tops, although beneath some a corner of an England shirt could be seen. They were striding purposefully and were clearly together. I heard cockney accents – a London firm looking for trouble and they'd been given the excuse.

It was two in the morning when we got back to our car. John's experiences, however, were just beginning.

The unfurnished cell provided little comfort, as the hard stone floor absorbed any body heat from me, and I spent a relatively sleepless night in cell 7b.

Sandwiches were provided at around 9.30 am, but this is an approximate time as all watches had been confiscated. There were no vegetarian sandwiches, and liquid refreshment was still only water. We were told we would be deported, yet the only reply to when was always 'two hours'.

At around 4.40pm on the Sunday afternoon, we were offered a shower, but were told we would be flying out in 20 minutes. Not wanting to miss this exit opportunity, most of the cell inhabitants declined.

At around 5 pm, 14 hours after being booked in, the British Consul arrived, but offered little comfort. We had no hot food, my medical condition remained untreated due to inadequate medical facilities, we could not use the phone, and still had no definite departure date. I managed to get in a question, requesting the Consul if he could allow us to stay. He said this would not be possible. He left, but our situation had not improved. The lads who had been in the same cell since Friday, were eventually called out for transport home.

We were then told we would all be allowed out to get some fresh air, before being returned to the cell. In fact, we were placed in a cell in a worse condition than the original one, already containing 15 men. Some of these were Travel Club members, had tickets for the game, and had been 'lifted' before getting to Charleroi. These men were not criminals. They were honest, intelligent and knowledgeable people, who were obviously incapable of mass civil unrest. Their stories of 'capture' were remarkably similar to my own. Our main objective now was to get home.

For me this came at around midnight, 22 hours after first being detained. I was called to the waiting area, ordered to sign three 'release' forms, but was refused a copy, being told one would be handed out once airborne. The policeman who checked my possessions and recuffed me was very polite, and was a credit to any police force. Unfortunately, and to my own shame, I felt so distressed at this point I could only muster a meek 'Thank you' when he put me on the bus. Prior to take-off, I had a stomach attack caused by the lack of medication and poor diet sustained over the past two days incarceration, but with reasonable compassion, I was allowed to leave the plane, and take off was delayed.

Upon landing in Manchester, I gave my details to the Greater Manchester Police, and was allowed home. I spent several hours travelling back to Maidstone, at considerable expense, only to find I may not be allowed to return to Holland to collect my possessions, or to Belgium to follow my club or my country.

We studied the Brussels map in the early hours (a day earlier than John finally made it home), looking for the most direct route out of town. A fellow fan was retching up his beer intake of the past, I imagine, three or four days. To call him sick as a dog, could only have been true if you had managed to find a dog with the ill health brought on by a diet of tripe, whisky and slug pellets, whilst suffering dysentery. You get the picture.

Anyway, at the end of this great day for English football, I also felt sick to my stomach.

Thanks for that, Ali.

Charleroi

Sunday 18th & Monday 19th June

AFTER SUCH AN emotional and traumatic experience as the long-awaited victory over Germany, which had rekindled hopes and even given rise to expectations of further progress in the tournament, the obvious thing to do would be to have a chilled day. Relax. A long lie-in, leisurely lunch, perhaps a trip out somewhere before finding a friendly bar with a telly to watch the evening games.

Unfortunately, Sunday for us was high pressure, a fanzine-writing day. Early start, and as it turned out, a late finish. And in the meantime lots of creativity and editorial judgement required.

Some sensitive decisions had to be taken. Was Kevin Keegan's morale high enough for us to be able to publish another back page of the highly amusing gibberish he occasionally he came out with in the media? We took our responsibilities in this area very seriously. How could we live with ourselves if a copy of our fanzine fell into his hands just before a big game and had a negative effect? Imagine the backlash against us if in a tear-filled television interview the great man sobbed 'I just couldn't motivate the lads any more; my spirit was crushed when I saw the FSA fanzine had been taking the mickey out of me.'

We'd taken all of this into consideration when producing the previous issue. We'd seen how disappointed he'd looked after the Portugal game, and decided we just couldn't risk it. So instead for that issue we'd used a selection of similar nonsense from other great names associated with England. We even thought that if Kevin Keegan saw these, he might perhaps be reinvigorated to know that he wasn't the only one capable of talking bollocks, and none of his predecessors had even been sacked for it. Well, except for his immediate predecessor, and that was slightly different.

So in issue two, we'd printed:

15 Pearls of Wisdom from England's Finest

1 'We didn't underestimate them. They were a lot better than we thought.' *BOBBY ROBSON*

2 'Once Tony Daley opens his legs you've got a problem.' *HOWARD WILKINSON*

3 'Playing with wingers is more effective against European sides like Brazil than English sides like Wales.' *RON GREENWOOD*

4 'If history is going to repeat itself I should think we can expect the same thing again.' *TERRY VENABLES*

5 'He's very fast and if he gets a yard ahead of himself nobody will catch him.' *BOBBY ROBSON*

6 'We're taking 22 players to Italy, sorry, to Spain . . . where are we, Jim?' *BOBBY ROBSON, on whether Paul Gascoigne should have gone to the 1998 World Cup – in France*

7 'If they hadn't scored, we might have got a better result.' *HOWARD WILKINSON*

8 'I never predict anything and I never will do.' *PAUL GASCOIGNE*

9 'At times he gave us what Barnes and Waddle could have given us but couldn't because they didn't play.' *BOBBY ROBSON*

10 'With hindsight, the biggest mistake I think I made was in not getting Eileen Drewery out to join us in France from the start.' *GLENN HODDLE*

11 'The Belgians were just standing around looking at each other, and that's no remedy for success.' *CHRIS WADDLE*

12 'Compared to the preparation Brazil have had, we are motorways behind them, absolute motorways. Still, it's no use crying over spilt milk, we'll just have to get a new cow.' *GLEN HODDLE*

13 'In football, time and space are the same thing.' *GRAHAM TAYLOR*

14 'What can I say about Peter Shilton? Peter Shilton is Peter Shilton, and he has been Peter Shilton since the year dot.' *BOBBY ROBSON*

15 'The beauty of Cup football is that Jack always has a chance of beating Goliath.' *TERRY BUTCHER*

Very amusing. But now we faced a different situation. The England camp must be buoyant, and Keegan looked ecstatic after the Germany game. Far from demoralising him, another selection of Keegan quotes would probably contribute to the party atmosphere in the team hotel in Spa, allowing the coach to demonstrate his ability to laugh at himself as he prepares his squad for the final group game. So issue number three, we decided, would hit the streets with a back page reading:

Wise Words From Our Great Leader (part 2)

13 more sayings of Kevin Keegan

1 'He's using his strength and that is his strength, his strength.'

2 'Gary always weighed up his options, especially when he had no choice.'

3 'Chile have three options – they could win or they could lose.'

4 'I'd love to be a mole on the wall in the Liverpool dressing room at half-time.'

5 'There's no job in football I've ever wanted. This is the only job in football I've ever wanted.'

6 'Mark Hughes at his very best: he loves to feel people right behind him.'

7 'We can't all be the general. Someone's got to stand on the pavement and watch as the generals go by.'

8 'The substitute is about to come on – he's a player who was left out of the starting line-up today.'

9 'The ref was vertically 15 yards away.'

10 'He can't speak Turkey, but you can tell he's delighted.'

11 'There'll be no siestas in Madrid tonight.'

12 'Despite his white boots, he has real pace . . .'

13 'There is only one other place in Europe on offer
   – everybody else will have to catch the ferry next
   season.'

Looking back, we obviously should have clocked the fact
that for issues one and three, in other words for the games
England lost, we used lists of thirteen quotes. All that time
spent agonising over the impact on the manager's morale, and
we overlooked something as obvious as that. The poor team
didn't stand a chance after we inadvertently jinxed them.

Strange, the role that superstitions play in football, and all
the bizarre rituals that have developed – like the players that
insist on putting their kit on in a certain order, or in running
out of the tunnel and onto the pitch first, or last, or third, or
whatever. And they're often taken very seriously. There must
be cases recorded of a manager who has unwittingly lumbered
himself with a selection dilemma by signing a second player
who insists on being last onto the pitch.

Some superstitions are more well-founded though. Watch
Shaka Hislop if ever the teams have to swap ends as a result
of the toss before a match. He won't run straight down the
middle of the field, he'll run round the outside. Apparently this
is because he once watched a game where in this situation the
goalkeepers passed each other in the centre circle and instead
of shaking hands, one keeper belted the other one, entirely
unseen, and knocked him out cold. Shaka's strategy is not
really a superstition, if you ask me, more a wise precaution.
And you'll notice, it's always worked for him. He's never yet
spent the last two minutes before a Premiership kick-off being
revived with smelling salts in the centre circle.

Though goalkeepers are notorious for superstitions, partly because they're just about all certifiably mad, there are exceptions. The great Peter Shilton once told me (once being also the total number of times I've talked to him, incidentally) that he had no time for superstitions at all. But he did always put his gloves one foot behind his right hand post, every game he played.

Back at the fanzine production table, we also produced another quiz (answers p.229):

The Even Lower Down Quiz – 3

1 Name three English clubs whose names include swear words.

2 There are five English clubs whose names include the letter x. Name them.

3 Who links the Munich air-crash and the winner of a UEFA Cup medal this year?

4 Who recently bought RSC Charleroi?

5 There are six players who have played for, and scored for, four clubs who were in the Premier League at the time. Name the players.

6 What can't you do at Hull City that you can do at any other club?

7 What's the connection between Hagi and Popescu?

8 Who scored the winning goal for Rumania last time England played them? (He's since had a television programme named after him.)

9 Name the former Everton, Sheffield Wednesday and

Newcastle United player whose father Olly was a
Hollywood film star.

10 Who captained England at cricket and played striker for
Scotland at football?

In the middle of all this frivolity we started getting phone calls
about UEFA's announcement of their intention to throw the
England team out of the tournament in the event of any more
trouble involving England fans.

I must admit, at first I thought this was a wind-up.
Everybody else in Belgium seemed to be having a day off,
so this had to be some bored journalists making their own
entertainment, taking the mickey out of the media-friendliness
of the FSA by inviting us to comment on something that hadn't
happened. A bit like the famous Chris Morris spoof, when he
got public figures to speak out about the threat posed to the
nation's youth by the fictional drug 'cake'.

But by the time I'd spoken to a couple of journalists who
I knew and trusted, and who seemed sober and on duty,
I realised that it was true. They wanted to know what I
thought.

I gave my immediate reaction based on what I'd seen and
heard over the previous few days, and my gut reaction as a
football fan. I was aware even then that I was very close to
events, that I was feeling quite involved personally, and that
the whole thing might conceivably look very different from
home. Apart from the people on the spot working on the
fanzine, I didn't have time to consult many people in the FSA
either, so I just made the best job of it that I could and called
it as I saw it.

I must admit though that weeks later, after the fuss has
died down, the heat and emotion have subsided, and I am

back at home, my attitude towards UEFA's position has not altered one iota. And having also since gone through the not particularly surprising experience of the decision about the 2006 World Cup hosts, if anything I feel reinforced in my initial suspicion that this announcement about Euro 2000 had far more to do with FIFA politics than it had to do with any genuine attempts to find a solution to the problems of English hooliganism.

This decision didn't make sense to me on any level. The UEFA spokesperson who I heard interviewed about it made some passing comment to the effect that 'the hooligans are not interested in the football, they're just here to cause trouble'. Now as I've already mentioned, I'm not sure I agree with that, but the point is, he said it. So based on that premise, what on earth is the point of imposing a football punishment? If they're not interested, why should that make any difference to them?

The exclusion of the team would be an unprecedented and heavy punishment − but it would impact on the team, the coach and the genuine supporters more than anyone else. As far as I was aware, no one had reported seeing Kevin Keegan, Alan Shearer or Tony Adams chucking patio furniture around Charleroi. Jacques van Gompel, the mayor of Charleroi, had said 'Most of the English fans behaved well'; he *didn't* continue '. . . so throw them and their team out of the tournament'. UEFA had contrived to come up with a measure that would according to their own estimation have little impact on the guilty, but would surpass even the efforts of the Belgian riot police in making life miserable for the innocent. Victory on a plate to the hooligans.

Not only was the UEFA announcement unjust in that respect, it was also inequitable in that it was so one-sided and selective. No doubt the structures of UEFA contain some arcane and complicated decision making processes that need to be by-passed if there are quick decisions to be made. But the decision here involved a significant change in policy, and yet it seems that the constituent member of UEFA which would bear the immediate brunt of it was not even consulted.

The previous policy of UEFA had always been that teams, clubs and national associations should not be held responsible for actions outside their immediate sphere of influence and away from the stadia. Now I'm not saying that I necessarily agree with that approach. I think that such is the importance of the sport in so many societies today, economically and culturally, that perhaps football clubs and authorities should think about what further impact they can have outside their own direct area of operation. But that's not really the point here. The fact remains that UEFA had held firm to their line even in very recent incidents – such as the tragic murder of the two Leeds fans in Istanbul, and the disturbances in Copenhagen at the UEFA Cup final. There had been no decision to punish or ban Galatasary, and no big fuss about it either, because it was generally accepted as custom and practice. By all means open up a debate, even initiate moves to reverse the policy – but to do an about-turn so quickly and in such circumstances suggested other motives.

And then, even if it was acceptable to change policy like that, surely it could only be done if the new policy applied equally and evenly to all the competing countries? Why was England being singled out for this treatment? Did the Belgian fans arrested after the opening game not come into this equation? Or any of the other nationalities involved in disturbances? And in particular, what about Turkey? Turkish fans had carried out at least one stabbing, of an English fan, and had been involved in more than their share of disturbances on the streets. Why was all that ignored? It is interesting that when UEFA a week or so later published the 'Fair Play' league table for the tournament, two teams were excluded, not for their conduct on the pitch but for the behaviour of their fans off it. The two countries 'relegated' were England and Turkey. But for this decision, England were singled out.

I feared the worst. Making England alone the scapegoats for the violence played directly into the hands of the racists, who had already been whipping up anti-Turkish sentiment and stoking up the 'everyone hates us, we don't care' feeling. To me, it also seemed to send out a clear invitation to the hooligans of any other country – and they all have them – to try to provoke the English. Either they won't be able to fight back, or if they do, their team will be thrown out of the tournament. It could have been disastrous.

Changing pages as we went along, we tried to reflect this in the fanzine. It struck us that somebody needed to try to speak up for the ordinary supporters. They'd come out with all the right intentions and been part of a fantastic occasion in Eindhoven. They'd overcome the disappointment of losing to Portugal, been buoyed by the win over Germany, and looked forward to the prospect of reaching the quarter-finals by at least drawing with Romania. Now this was jeopardised by a combination of the thugs and the authorities running the whole event.

We also tried to take up the issue of racism. We'd noticed that there seemed to be a much stronger undercurrent of racism among the England fans than we had encountered two years earlier in the World Cup in France. This was bound up for many by the anti-Turkish sentiment that had been building over the last few months. I talked to a lot of fans about this, and came across some very contradictory attitudes. Most people were disgusted by it, and were perfectly capable of remembering that the great majority of Turks and

Turkish football fans condemned the events in Istanbul and Copenhagen.

At the other end of the spectrum were out-and-out, fully conscious racists. They hate all foreigners, and a fair proportion of Englishmen too. Their racism is a constant feature of their existence. Some of them went as far as to produce stickers proclaiming their presence. One sticker, of which I took great pleasure in taking down several copies from walls and door frames in Charleroi, read: ENGLISH VOLUNTEER FORCE, above a badly designed swastika. To the left was the (ironic? Can these people do irony?) phrase 'Fucking Racists!'; to the right, the words 'Charlton Athletic .F.C' (sic – you can't really expect people with this level of intelligence to get the punctuation right). Across the bottom: WHITE POWER.

There were more of these organised fascists about than I'd come across for quite a while around football, and there had also been the odd press report about Combat 18 members being prevented from travelling into Belgium in the first place. These are – without exception in my experience – very unpleasant, violent people, and not just football but the whole of society would be best rid of them. They are still a small minority among England followers though, and it's probably worth registering too that they are not really open to persuasion about the error of their ways.

The biggest challenge to anti-racists is how to marginalise these people and cut them off from the rest of the fans, to minimise their pernicious influence. The biggest change I noticed at Euro 2000 compared to the World Cup two years previously was the increase in the number of other travelling fans who while not part of this group of organised fascists, were prepared to be led and influenced by them.

It was among this crowd that the Turkish issue featured most prominently. Some of this lot, while not organised in any way, were already very racist, and took great pleasure in racist songs and abuse. But there were others I talked to who were open to discussion about things, and who vehemently denied being racist – they just hated the Turks. There was even one black bloke among a group I talked to adopting this attitude. Their argument went that they had no problem with blacks, or even Asians (one bloke even said that he thought that Asian people would like the song "I'd rather be a Paki than a Turk", which I couldn't quite follow). But the Turks were violent thugs, out to get the English – look what they'd done in Istanbul.

I had some interesting discussions with some of these fans. Some clearly weren't going to be persuaded easily; others were prepared to engage and follow the argument. What did strike me though was that we wouldn't get past first base in trying to break these people from racist attitudes if we hadn't already won some credibility among them as football fans by offering practical assistance. By being prepared to stick up for the innocent fans, when the easier option being adopted by most of the media and all the politicians was to lump everyone in together, also meant that we could get their ear to tackle difficult issues.

I found that talking about the failure of the Belgian police to differentiate between ordinary fans and hooligans led quite easily in to the failure of others, England fans included, to differentiate between ordinary Turks and the hooligan element of their community. It began to dawn on some of the English fans that the genuine fear they felt as they walked down some of the streets of Brussels, of being attacked at random just because they were English, had given them a fleeting glimpse of what life must be like for many black and Asian people on the streets of Britain every day.

Getting people to talk about different kinds of Turks at

least began to get them to think of them as people, rather than as one hostile mass.

I also talked to quite a few Turks, both in Eindhoven and in Charleroi. They talked about problems they had with a minority of their own community, who were being whipped up into an ever more extreme nationalist attitude, again some of it consciously done by organised groups such as the Grey Wolves. One Turk was quoted in the English press along similar lines: 'There are a small number of people on both sides who want to cause trouble. There is a Turkish expression, "The fly is little but it can cause a lot of problems".' They also stressed that in their communities people were aware that most English fans were fine, that the hostile racist ones were a minority; the problem was they couldn't tell the difference by looking at them. The worst thugs were easy to identify – they were the ones chanting racist songs and giving Nazi salutes. But the others – it was impossible, they said, to tell the difference between an ordinary fan and a racist thug who just wasn't doing anything at that moment. So their general instinct had been to keep well clear of the English, though there were limitations to how far this was possible when the English came to their town. The ones actively seeking out the English were more likely to be looking for trouble, in the process reinforcing all the prejudices the English had about the Turks.

I was particularly struck by one encounter I had with a group of young Turks very soon after we'd arrived in Charleroi. We had just parked the embassy van in the square and were setting our stall out, when half-a-dozen young lads, maybe fifteen years old, began to assemble behind us. I went across to talk to them, and most of them legged it. I spoke in French to one of the two lads who stayed; more than anything else, he looked terrified. He'd clearly been told, among other things, that the English don't speak French, but once he believed that I was indeed English, he asked if I was a hooligan. He didn't look entirely convinced when I said no, and nervously told me he was Turkish, seeming to brace himself for a violent reaction. He laughed when I asked if he was a hooligan himself, and the ice was broken. We chatted for a while about football, and his mates returned and joined in. I gave him some FA key rings, which chuffed him to bits, and he went off with his mates to report back about what the English were really like. I couldn't help feeling both pleased and sad; pleased that he'd gone off happy, but sad that his expectations had been so low.

As well as the anti-racist content within the fanzine, we also had to do new versions of our regular features. One popular item had been the Wordsearches, so we devised a new, highly topical one on the theme of the Belgian police.

The Belgian Police Wordsearch

```
I  N  D  I  S  C  R  I  M  I  N  A  T  E  N
D  N  N  O  E  H  C  N  U  R  T  D  E  I  O
C  P  J  D  D  R  I  P  Z  A  O  M  A  D  N
H  U  D  E  Y  O  N  E  Z  B  R  I  R  O  N
E  R  E  Z  C  H  O  M  L  I  I  N  G  L  A
C  P  D  A  N  T  I  U  E  D  O  I  A  P  C
K  L  N  R  E  L  T  C  S  N  P  S  S  C  R
S  E  A  C  C  I  C  S  C  O  C  T  O  V  E
P  H  H  R  A  F  A  E  L  B  I  R  R  E  T
R  E  Y  E  L  S  E  S  U  B  D  A  B  K  A
A  L  V  W  P  N  R  R  E  O  R  T  A  C  W
Y  M  A  O  M  O  R  O  N  R  G  I  P  A  R
I  E  E  P  O  T  E  H  T  R  E  V  O  T  A
N  T  H  B  C  A  V  O  A  R  R  E  S  T  S
G  X  A  C  A  B  O  X  T  N  E  S  B  A  H
```

It's always a pleasant feeling when you subsequently discover that your efforts have been appreciated, and I got exactly that reward when on Tuesday, a few hours before the Romania game kicked off, I passed a minibus full of Belgian riot police parked in a side street. To a man, they were all trying to do the Belgian Police Wordsearch.

We completed the fanzine in the small hours again – compiling a fanzine seems to be one of those jobs that always expands to fill all the time available, then needs a couple of hours more to finish it – and most of my co-workers went off to bed. The team was staying a few kilometres outside Charleroi in what resembled a building site. I can best describe it by saying that if a few more thousand pounds is invested in it, then it could eventually be upgraded to youth hostel standard. Cathy and I stayed in town, crashing at a building set aside for use as the German Fans' Embassy. We needed to be up early to make sure that we e-mailed the copy of the fanzine we had just completed to the Dutch printers.

A straightforward job. I was booked to do a live interview for Radio Five Live at what felt like a couple of hours before the crack of dawn, so we took the disks and borrowed a BBC laptop to send the fanzine files off. Sorted – or so we thought, until we got a phone call an hour or two later from the printers, asking where the copy was. It hadn't arrived.

A surreal few hours followed, in which Cathy and I tried every possible internet connection we could find in order to send the bloody fanzine, and all in the grip of exhaustion after two long days without much sleep.

In the middle of all this, I did an interview for *Panorama*, struggling to stay awake under the lights in a hotel bedroom for an hour to produce the two minutes they eventually used. If you thought I looked dopey on that programme, you were right, and now you know why.

We persevered all day with the e-mail attempts, until Cathy cracked and had to go to get some kip. I decided to give it one last try. One of the Belgian fan coaches arranged for me to use an internet resource centre for local young people, so I went there and turfed some poor Walloon teenager off his terminal and got started. Three-quarters of an hour later, I'd successfully sent the first page via the slowest computer I'd ever encountered. It was now four o'clock in the afternoon; at this rate I'd finish sending all sixteen pages early the next morning. I finally admitted defeat, and phoned the printers to tell them.

"Hello, it's Kevin from the FSA. I'm phoning about the fanzine."

"Oh yes. It's all going fine. It will be delivered tomorrow lunchtime"

"But you said it hadn't arrived!"

"Oh, it came a little later. Didn't you know?"

Apparently the very first attempt, via the BBC, had eventually come through after all. The problem had been at the printers' end. I didn't know whether to laugh or cry, so I went to sleep.

Charleroi

Tuesday 20th June

I'M PLEASED TO say that the day of the Romania game dawned later for me than most days had. I strolled, in bright sunshine, to the square late in the morning and found it slowly filling up with England fans.

It was a very different scene from how I remembered Saturday though. Gone were the oppressive numbers of police on the one hand, and the threatening, chanting Englishmen on the other. There were uniformed police in groups of half-a-dozen, discreetly but visibly posted around the square. There were plenty of England fans too, enjoying the sunshine, tying their flags to trees and lampposts. There was the occasional chant, too, but nothing more sinister than 'Ing-er-lund'. Mellow seemed the best word to describe the atmosphere.

I stand by all I've said about the UEFA threat to expel England from the tournament, but I would concede that it appeared to be a factor in the behaviour of many of the England fans on the Tuesday. Many of the unpleasant characters that had blighted the square on Saturday simply didn't seem to be there, fortunately as they would have been unlikely to have modified their behaviour for anybody. So it was probably people who wouldn't have caused problems anyway who were the most affected by the threat of expulsion.

These people were on their best behaviour, as though they'd gone for tea at their posh auntie's and had been warned by their parents beforehand to make a good impression.

The poor people who seemed to suffer most as a consequence were the modest numbers of Romanians who arrived early in the day. Distinctive in their bright yellow shirts, they were plagued by England fans desperate to shake their hands, or worse, hug and kiss them, in an outward display of friendship. God only knows what they told the folks back in Bucharest about their encounter with the feared English. Not what their mates back home would be expecting.

'We saw the riots in Charleroi on the telly – what were they like, the English?'

'I was surrounded by a group of six of them outside a bar . . .'

'Yes?'

'They wore no shirts, they had big bellies and lots of tattoos . . .'

'Yes?'

'They had been drinking beer since early in the morning, and they all came up to me . . .'

'Yes?'

'And then they kissed me and gave me a T-shirt.'

There was a total absence of anything threatening about the mood. The media were out in force again, but there was something half-hearted even about them, as if they too didn't think anything would happen. I gave an interview to Sky News, and I was still on their third floor balcony looking down on the square when I saw the nearest thing there was to an incident all day. A troop of maybe eight Belgian police marched across the square, grabbed a bloke wearing long trousers but no shirt who was standing beside an England flag, asked a couple of questions of a bloke in shorts beside him and hauled Long Trousers off. The crowd looked on curiously for a moment and then continued about their business.

I was curious myself as to what had happened, so on my way back to the van I stopped for a chat with the bloke in shorts the police had spoken to. His name was Alan, and he was a Manchester City fan. The other bloke had come up to him earlier when he was trying to tie up his flag to a tree, had taken out his boot lace and given it to him to secure one side of the flag. Alan had chatted to him for a few minutes, without a high degree of communication taking place, as the bloke was a local who didn't speak much English, and left again, with Alan feeling if anything fairly well disposed towards him. A few minutes later he'd come back to Alan, said a few more words to him, then suddenly started Sieg Heiling at a passing Turk. Alan was actually in the middle of a call on his mobile at the time, and didn't quite grasp what was going on. Suddenly he saw a troop of Belgian policemen coming towards him, and he froze. They grabbed the local Nazi, saying that he was well-known to them as a local troublemaker, but they had some questions for Alan too. Apparently they had been watching their man for a while, had seen him and Alan chatting, and then seen Alan making a call on his mobile. Naturally (?) they drew the conclusion that Alan was an English Nazi hooligan rallying his forces on the phone after receiving local information. Only the timely arrival of Alan's wife Angela had saved Alan and his Man City flag being nicked.

But just when we thought the whole day might go off without any problems at all, we heard the news that the mayor of Brussels had played his joker.

There had been some trouble in the capital the evening before, the undisputed version of events being that England fans drinking in a couple of bars had been attacked by local

Turkish fans 'celebrating' their victory over the host nation and their progress into the knockout stage. Windows had been smashed, one or two relatively minor injuries had been sustained, but the England fans had barricaded themselves into the bars and refused to retaliate. Backed up in their version of events by the bar owners – Thierry de Groot, owner of the Pot Carre bar told reporters, 'The English were totally faultless. They had been drinking quietly then the Turkish stormed the bar' – the fans were naturally angry, a mood that increased when the mayor issued a statement about the incident – blaming them on the English.

M. Francois-Eavier de Donnea, as the mayor is called (he will want his name remembered, it is election year after all, which might explain a lot) said, 'There were still people looking for English hooligans for revenge. They still feel they were psychologically attacked by British hooligans. It was not a good idea to provoke them. It started a chain reaction that was hard to stop.' Any offence that may understandably have been caused among England fans who had not caused any trouble at the weekend and who were innocent victims of attack on Monday evening was then compounded by the words of Gerhard Aigner. Yes, that's right, the same Gerhard Aigner who as chief executive of UEFA had threatened to expel England from the tournament. He described the events in Brussels, in which Turkish hooligans threw concrete slabs and iron bars through the windows of bars where English and Belgian fans were drinking together, as 'a joyful party' that went wrong.

To their credit, the England fans I met all restricted their anger to the spoken word, describing both the above quoted authority figures as 'hypocrites'. But then M. de Donnea's masterstroke was played. He ordered the cancellation of all trains back to Brussels from Charleroi after the end of the

Romania game. To complicate things even further, he ordered that the replacement bus service could only be used by English fans if they could prove that they had accommodation in Brussels. To 'assist' this process, every hotel in Brussels was instructed to issue England fans staying with them with a voucher, which the mayor's office was going to supply.

Even at its best, this idea would be a bureaucratic nightmare. And it was not at its best. For a start, it ignored the needs of those fans who wanted to travel to somewhere north of Brussels, who were relying on changing trains in the capital. Not only did their first train no longer exist, they would not be allowed to board the replacement buses. Anybody who came to Charleroi first, perhaps arriving from Eindhoven where they'd watched the Sweden-Italy match, could no longer complete their journey to Brussels, but would be forced to stay without advance notice in the town which enjoyed the least hotel accommodation of all the host cities.

And then there was the problem of the England fans who did have accommodation in Brussels. Those fans in other words that the mayor *was* prepared to countenance returning to his city. Many of them arrived in Charleroi early that morning, and the first they'd heard of the voucher system was when we told them about it. Their hotels had told them nothing about it. In many cases the hotels knew nothing about it, or weren't issued with vouchers by the mayor's office until later in the day, after the fans had travelled. I met one couple, Dan and Jo, who had paid in advance for their £100 a night hotel room, followed the advice they'd been given and brought with them only their passports, their match tickets and the cash they needed for the day, leaving everything else in the hotel safe. Now they faced a night on the streets of Charleroi, waiting for the first train in the morning.

*   *   *

Confusion over this issue reigned all day. We were involved in constant negotiations with various authorities trying to talk some sense into them. As the day went on, it became clear that none of the other Belgian authorities agreed with the mayor's decision. The mayor of Charleroi was furious – it was in effect dumping any potential problem on his doorstep, and compounding it too. The police weren't impressed – they were going to have to deal with the mess it left behind. The British consular authorities clearly weren't impressed either. All sorts of meetings went on all day trying to sort it out. At one stage we were informed that the Belgian interior ministry was suggesting that our fans' embassy take on the job of informing England fans of what was happening (which we were doing anyway), and that any fans unable to get back to their hotels could be directed to us to have the bad news explained to them. We declined this particular offer – why should we get all the grief for a decision that we didn't agree with in the first place?

Nonetheless, the longest queue we had at the van all day was when the new fanzine arrived and people came to get their copies, which was gratifying. The mood generally stayed positive all day; my mood started well thanks to a decent sleep, and improved no end when I received my first perk of the job, an official accreditation as a 'fan coach' which gave me access to the stadium for the match.

Ah, yes, the match. What a mixture of emotions. Great atmosphere to start with, dampened by Chivu's goal halfway through the first half. Then the euphoria as it turned around to 2–1 by half-time. I had a feeling it couldn't be that easy, and the lead was short-lived. Four minutes of the second half, in fact. But then the game went on, and of course a draw was enough for us. We were so close to going through. Then Philip Neville. Philip bloody Neville.

Words to that effect were the constant muttered refrain for the full length of the walk back to the station after the game. I learnt subsequently that at half-time – that short interlude when England were still winning – yet another meeting had taken place among all the various authorities involved in the decisions about getting people back to Brussels. Well, nearly all the authorities. As I was told the story, they waited until the representative of the mayor of Brussels had gone home, then reconvened. Amazingly at the last session, all insistence on possession of a voucher being a requirement for boarding a bus to Brussels had disappeared. We divided our embassy forces between the South railway station, where the trains would have been going from, and the West railway station, where the buses were going from, to spread the good news.

Chaos still prevailed, but on a much lesser scale than it would otherwise have done, had that last meeting not taken place. The plan before that meeting had been to let people without vouchers onto the buses, but not if they had been drinking or had tattoos. I wouldn't have fancied having to police that one.

Post-England

The Quarter Finals

THE HANGOVER THAT Philip Neville caused didn't really last too long. Emotional farewells to most of the team, who were on their way home – no England fans, thus no embassy service required. Four or five were to stay until the quarter-final weekend, then I'd be on my own. My brief was, working alongside the Dutch and Belgian fan coaches, to 'observe' the rest of the tournament, and to do what I could in the interests of England fans, whether they be the ones coming to watch the remaining games as neutrals, or the ones arrested and deported already. In the process I might even get to take in a few matches myself. There are worse ways to earn a living, I suppose.

Straight back into the swing of the tournament, then; hair of the dog, to stretch the hangover analogy even further. Ali and I headed for Arnhem to catch the game between Norway and Slovenia.

We went by car. The traffic was bad, so we were late arriving. I followed signs on the motorway for the football car parks. Well, it seemed like a good idea at the time. The Dutch are generally good at the whole 'Park and Ride' business, and the theory behind it is great. You drive to a car park on the outskirts of town, leave your car and get on a bus, which drops you right beside the stadium. Simple. Except when they plan the timetable for the buses, they work on the not entirely unreasonable assumption that people wanting to go to the match will want to be at the stadium by half-an-hour before kick-off, at the latest. So that's when the buses stop. Not a lot of use though if you are late.

A 'Park and Ride' car park after the last bus has gone ceases to be a 'Park and Ride' car park. It becomes a field with cars in it. Of course you soon suss out that there's not a soul around, and there's not much point in waiting on the off chance that there'll be another bus before the league season starts. So you head off again in the direction of the stadium. Or you would, if you knew what direction the stadium was in.

The 'Park and Ride' car parks are very well signed on the way in. On the way out, they're quite well signed back out again, back to where you came from. But there's not a single sign towards the stadium. Why should there be? The bus drivers know the way – they're locals, and they're professional drivers. And car drivers don't need to know the way, because they won't be driving, they'll be leaving their cars behind and taking the bus. That's the whole point of a 'Park and Ride' scheme after all, isn't it?

So it was half-time by the time we reached the stadium. We were slightly comforted by the fact that there was no score, less so by the news that it had been a crap game thus far. We looked for our seats, but there was really no need, as there were thousands empty. We found an almost empty row, where we only had to pass two other people on the end of the row to get in. It turned out they were English fans, Adrian Rees and Chris Stokes. In a strange perversion of the usual order of things, Adrian told me he was a Luton season ticket holder living in Manchester.

The second-half was no better than the first was reported

to be. The atmosphere in the horrible indoor Gelredome (the roof was at least open this time) was, well, European. Quite jolly and cheerful, enthusiastic more than passionate. The Slovenians were fun to watch, as they bounced up and down like a thousand Tiggers in replica shirts. As they unfurled over their heads a big flag of the kind banned in English stadia as a 'fire hazard', the Norwegians applauded appreciatively.

It stayed nil–nil till the bitter end. Solskjaer missed a sitter or two, which was nice. Eirik Bakke came on as a substitute, much to the delight of Ali, a Leeds fan, and went off injured again eighteen minutes later, much to the delight of me, a miserable bastard. At the end of the game, there was an announcement that the Yugoslavs were currently beating Spain 3–2, meaning that Norway would go through to the quarter-finals, so the Norwegian fans went home happy. Or at least as far as their cars, as they would no doubt then discover on the radio that the Spaniards had scored twice in injury time to win 4–3, meaning that they went through instead of Norway. Life can be cruel.

We raced back from Arnhem to meet the others at the fan coaches' 'base camp' near Tilburg, in time to catch most of the group game between Holland and France. Both teams were already through, though the Dutch still had the incentive of playing Yugoslavia on home soil in Rotterdam, rather than Spain in Bruges. The French didn't seem that bothered who they played next or where, as they put out their reserves, but they still made a game of it, twice taking the lead before going down to the 'odd goal in five', as the papers say.

I enjoyed all this while devouring the largest selection of Chinese take-away food I'd ever seen, drinking bottled beer and throwing shoes at mice. Happy times.

The next two days were strange, in that there was no football on. We had plenty to do, not least putting more reports and stuff onto the website we were providing in conjunction with Football365. We also launched a campaign to try to do something about all the fans who had been innocently deported from Belgium.

Back home the politicians were baying for somebody's blood, and demanding draconian new measures against football hooliganism. It never ceases to amaze me how some politicians will jump on a populist bandwagon without ever letting their absolute ignorance of the subject matter get in the way. I mean, has anybody ever seen Ann Widdecombe at an away game? Or at a game at all?

One of the measures being touted was legislation to give police the power to arrest and prevent from travelling abroad fans who had never been convicted of anything, just on the basis of a suspicion that they might be predisposed towards trouble, or look like they might be. Many of those who'd been deported not unreasonably feared that they may well end up on some government list of people to be banned from travelling to future matches, meaning they would effectively be punished twice for not doing anything wrong. We hoped that by highlighting some of their cases, we could draw attention to some of the potential injustices such legislation could cause. So we issued a press release to the media both at home and in Belgium and Holland asking affected fans to come forward, so we could prepare a comprehensive dossier to present to the Home Office.

We also wanted to stop the extension of banning orders to people who had not been convicted. I have no problem with combining the two forms of banning order, domestic and international, into one. It seems to me just to be clearing up an anomaly; why should someone deemed unfit to attend a football match at home be considered fit to travel abroad for games? But some of the new ideas under discussion included giving an individual police officer power to stop a football fan travelling if he didn't like the look of him. No conviction or court appearance required, therefore no opportunity to defend oneself. The first step towards a police state. And we'd already seen in Belgium what powers of arrest without any offence being committed could lead to.

Before anyone objects that I'm getting a bit carried away here, and insists that no-one would ever countenance powers of arrest on the basis of not liking someone's appearance, let me just quote you something I read in a Sabena Airlines in-flight magazine before Euro 2000 began. These are the words of Alain Courtois, the man in charge of tournament organisation in Belgium.

> *All fans are welcome, but we have a warning for trouble-makers. Belgium will be ruthless in implementing a special law allowing the police to detain for up to 12 hours anyone whose appearance gives cause for concern. For example, by showing tattoos, wearing overly-patriotic shorts or having a crew cut.*

I looked around me on the plane when I read that. Despite the restricted view as a result of the high seat backs, I could see at least three people who wouldn't be disembarking in Brussels if Alain had his way. And this was on a weekday business flight weeks before the tournament. I think this is all a bit over the top – and that's even allowing for the fact that there was probably a misprint in there. It probably meant overly-patriotic shirts, not shorts. They couldn't seriously intend to check people's underpants, could they? Could they?

The next couple of days without matches were spent in a more leisurely style. We took the printers out to lunch, to help them celebrate our mutual success in delivering the fanzine successfully. We went to a party held for all the fan coaches of all the competing countries, to mark the fact that most of them would be going home along with their country's team. You could tell it was a pan-European do, because the music was appalling.

Before we knew it, there were matches on again. I had been given a couple of tickets for the quarter final that England would have been in had it not been for Phil Neville, but was now between Italy and Romania, at the Roi Baudouin stadium in Brussels.

I'm not always desperately keen about matches as a neutral, though they're nearly always better than no matches at all. But at an international tournament, there's usually a sense of occasion about all of them, plus a feeling that you're privileged to be seeing some of the world's best players in a competitive game. Italy v Romania was, if Romania lost, to be Hagi's last ever international game, and it was a privilege to see him play live, especially since he'd missed the game against England. Still fantastically skilful, enormously influential on his team, yet sadly his last game for his country will be remembered most for his unnecessary sending-off.

The game was over as a contest by half-time, goals by Totti and Inzaghi wrapping it up, which meant that I could relax and watch the half-time entertainment.

I have a strange fascination with half-time entertainment, particularly at international tournaments. Clearly with time limited, they have to make an immediate impact. Not like opening ceremonies, which frankly frighten me. And if they do that to me, God knows what they do to kids. Imagine how sick you'd feel if you'd managed to encourage your recalcitrant four year old to come to a game, in the hope that it might be the beginning of being able to pass off your favourite pastime as contributing to childcare, and then the poor bairn gets the shit scared out of them by a strange shape in disturbing colours with no eyes, ears, nose or mouth lumbering towards them with obvious malicious intent. And that's the ones held in the stadia. The parades through the streets are even worse. The one in Paris in 1998 was led by a giant Footix, the World Cup mascot, or in other words by an enormous cock. Which frightened me, though I suppose it could be somebody's idea of a great night out.

Half-time entertainment has to be more instant, more compelling. At the England-Germany game, it consisted of a man called Alfred Reindel (I'm guessing at the spelling; he wasn't mentioned in the programme for some reason, so I'm going off the tannoy announcement). I gather he was a local lad which might account for some of the reception he got, but he was very capable at what he did. He was a ball juggler, a football juggler in fact. And if I understood the announcements correctly, he set a world record before my very eyes, and you don't see that very often.

His record was for juggling a football 150 times on his head in 30 seconds, quite an amazing achievement. Five times in a second is fast, too fast to see, you would have thought. If I had thought about it, I might have been less disappointed. I imagined him heading the ball way up into the air each time, like when normal people play keepy-up, but of course that was unrealistic. To head the ball five times a second for thirty seconds, the movement each time has to be almost imperceptibly small. It was still impressive, and I'm sure the record will stand for a long time, not least because I can't imagine many other people wanting to waste their lives practising. He looked like he was having some sort of twitching fit.

Still, that was more imaginative than Eindhoven, at half-time between Sweden and Turkey. There, in keeping with the hi-tech nature of the stadium owners, they showed a video and played the tournament theme song. And even that was better than the Gelredome for Norway–Slovenia – they didn't have any at all, presumably to encourage people to visit the shops and have time to change their money into bloody Ohras.

In Brussels though, there had clearly been a lot of thought put into the entertainment. Brains had no doubt been racked, but without coming up with any form of common denominator between Romanian and Italian culture. So there were two lots. First, for the Romanians, a violinist appeared. You could tell he was for the Romanians, as he was wearing a replica Romania shirt. He came on and fiddled for a bit, and was joined by people dressed in white overalls, topped off with red, yellow and blue hats. Their trouser legs were tucked into their boots, which I always think gives men a somewhat effeminate air, and they carried big sticks. They danced, a bit like Morris dancers but much, much faster, and about ten times more camp (if indeed it's possible to be more camp than a Morris dancer). They left the field to massive applause, albeit exclusively from the Romanians.

Then it was the Italians' turn. You could tell this one was for the Italians, partly by default I suppose, and partly by the fact that she 'sang' a song which seemed to be called 'Viva Italia', which was a bit of a give-away. Her hair had been bleached blonde, though clearly not recently, giving her the look of an Italian sub-Mel C. She had a 'backing band' consisting of two blokes with guitars and one with a keyboard slung low around his neck. All three 'musicians' let their instruments swing untouched while they clapped along to the 'singer'. It will be a sad loss to the culture of our continent if Eurovision ever sinks this low. They left the field to zero applause, but at least they had the good grace to look embarrassed and guilty.

Incidentally, it was also at this game that I saw the saddest looking fan of the whole tournament, and that was no mean achievement. Don't ever let anyone tell you the Italians have got natural style. This guy had on white overalls, which he seemed to have spray painted with red and green blotches. At random. In the dark. On his head he was wearing one of those novelty hats that just aren't funny any more − if they ever were − in the shape of an umbrella, onto which more blotches of spray paint had been added. Onto the back of it he'd sellotaped red, white and green crepe paper streamers. Very smart. I've just assumed he was supporting Italy, by the way, as I clearly wasn't going to go up to him and ask. If by any chance he wasn't, then he was most definitely the saddest looking fan.

At either end of the ground there was one of those inflatable figures in each team's colours which stood up when a blast of air was blown up it. Sadly despite the victory, the Italian one just didn't seem to be able to stay erect. Still, happens to us all some time, I suppose.

The second-half was less than rivetting, the Italians apparently not wanting to overexert themselves unnecessarily. Their 78th minute substitute, one Del Piero, came on to a massive cheer, and looked very lively. I remember thinking to myself, that might be one player who really makes a name for himself this tournament. I have an unerring eye for that sort of thing.

Next day the remaining members of the embassy team went home, and I was alone. Alone, but with tickets for the France v Spain quarter final in Bruges. I headed straight there, but I knew in advance that accommodation in Bruges would be very hard to come by, so on the way I called into Gent and found myself a hotel room. I also discovered while I was there that in the middle of Gent is situated the world's largest hanging basket. I mention this merely in case it ever comes up in a pub quiz. They'll be expecting people to look puzzled and guess 'Babylon' or something, but you can now impress your mates by saying quietly, 'Oh, I know this one. It was in that book.'

The world's largest hanging basket is sponsored by Fortis Bank. I mention this merely in case there's a supplementary question for a bonus point. You'd be cursing me if there was and I hadn't mentioned it, right?

I arrived in Bruges in plenty of time to find a bar and watch the Holland-Yugoslavia goal feast. I was in the company of a Belgian journalist from a socialist newspaper who'd phoned me to ask for an interview about the experiences of English football fans at the hands of the Belgian police. In an act of solidarity I gave him my spare match ticket.

We took the special Euro 2000 bus from the station to the stadium for the evening fixture. I say to the stadium but in fact from the dropping off point we still had a long walk to the ground, through a wealthy residential area. We arrived at the ground and took our seats in an uncovered corner with the sun directly in our eyes. Next to us were Adrian and Chris, the Luton fans I'd sat beside in Arnhem. Small world, this Euro 2000. I took in the scene as best I could, and soaked up the great atmosphere generated by the three sets of supporters.

As well as the Spanish and the French, there were a few thousand Dutch there too, and they were naturally cock-a-hoop, having just thrashed the Yugoslavs 6–1. The chants began to ring around the ground. First, accompanied by clapping, 'Espana'. Then, louder, 'Allez Les Bleus'. Then loudest of all, 'Patrick Kluivert', sung by Dutchmen standing up all over the stadium.

It was a great game to watch, on and off the pitch.

Two-one by half-time. At one point Zidane fluffed an easy chance; shortly afterwards France won a free kick and Zidane lined up to take it. Showing the sort of judgement which sets Luton's finest apart from the rest of us, Adrian turns to me and says "They're surely not letting Zidane take this after that cock-up". Seconds later, Canizares is picking the ball out of the net as Zidane's sweet free-kick gives France a one–nil lead.

The whole game was a spectacle. Apart from seeing some of the best players in Europe, the crowd were marvellous too; the French constantly loud, the Spanish colourful, and singing something to the tune of a song we used to sing at Newcastle. Our version was called 'Somebody's pinched my sombrero'; I got the impression that theirs might be a little bit less frivolous, and that it was probably their tune first.

A couple of other things amused me. The Dutch held a Mexican wave of their own. I don't like Mexican waves, but this one was funny, as only Dutchmen in orange seemed to join in, all round the stadium.

Then in the last minute, with Spain 2–1 down, they got a penalty. The 'ultras' behind the Spanish goal lit a red flare in premature celebration, and couldn't throw it over the back of the stand quickly enough when Raul missed the kick.

To The Final

I WAS BACK in Brussels for the semi-final between France and Portugal. Perhaps the only positive spin-off of all the problems there had been with English fans – and even this was a very limited positive, as it was only me that benefited – was that I was offered an official accreditation to go to the Brussels semi-final, on the basis that some 1,700 tickets had been sold to English fans. These were tickets sold by postal application or over the Internet for the neutral areas. I knew that these would be either fans who were genuinely not bothered which teams were competing, they just wanted to see a good semi-final, or they were wild-eyed optimists who thought there might be a chance that England would get that far. Either way, I was asked if I'd be there to help 'sort out any problems with the English', and I'm always willing to help.

Where to go in the stadium wasn't quite so easy to decide; it wasn't as straightforward as going where England were, as the English ticket holders were scattered all over. So I got my eye on one English flag and followed it. I'd already seen people following things, so it seemed a good idea. On one of the main streets in the centre of Brussels, I'd seen a smartly-dressed woman holding up a card saying 'Car 4 (Voiture 7)' and there was a whole procession of people following her. Then I'd encountered what looked to be a ceremonial 'March of the Sponsors'; a procession of Philips VIP card holders, then people with Coca Cola lollipop style placards leading a crocodile of people wearing French replica shirts.

I'd had a good look around the centre of Brussels before the game. There were crowds of drunken Frenchmen around many of the bars that the week before had been England territory, and the Frenchmen were singing too, but somehow there wasn't quite the same air of menace. The police had sealed off most of the entrances to the Grande Place, but the square itself was half full. Most of the drunken noise was coming from more of the many Dutchmen who seemed to have bought up tickets for every game – they were starting to irritate me by being everywhere. Apparently there had been 160 arrests after the Dutch quarter final, of which 100 had been in Rotterdam itself, but it hadn't made great headlines anywhere.

Inside the stadium perimeter, I discovered that having a credential with the words 'Fan Co-ordinator' on it might get me into the stadium, but it had its downside too. I became a point of contact for any madman with a problem. One bloke came up to me and asked for help in getting his plastic flagstick back from the steward who had confiscated it. I didn't hold out much hope and told him so, so he started telling me his life story. He was wearing a French shirt; he explained that he was not from France, but French was his mother tongue. He felt it was outrageous that he could be treated like this, what with him being an invalid and all. I almost started to feel sorry for him until he told me he was a war veteran, and then showed me his national flag he wished to hold aloft. It was Swiss. Funnily enough, he couldn't tell me what war he was a Swiss army veteran of.

Inside the stadium itself, whole blocks were again coloured orange; half of one end, an area as big as the French themselves had. It seemed I wasn't the only one getting sick of them; when they started up a chant of 'Holland, Holland', they were loudly booed from all sides.

I found myself a seat, which was not as easy as it sounds – my accreditation entitled me to access to the stadium, but not a seat. A jobsworth woman steward kept telling not to stand where I was, so I said I'd find an empty seat somewhere. She said she couldn't allow me to sit in empty seat; that would have to be authorised by a man in a red cap with a radio. So I just said fine, go and fetch him; if you want me, I'll just be sitting in that empty seat. Strangely, he never came.

I discovered I was sitting opposite the tunnel, in seats that had been allocated to a corporate group, the members of which were all wearing badges saying 'Prestige Restaurant'. My neighbour was a very charming Belgian from Gent, who chatted away to me in English. He explained that he didn't really like football, but had been invited by a company, and he quite liked the atmosphere. One advantage of sitting where I did was that none of this group were really into those bloody awful Mexican waves, so I could at least see all of the game.

A good game it was too. Portugal went ahead through Nuno Gomes, which prompted even louder singing from the impressive Portuguese fans. They were impressive, but they didn't seem to know many songs. There was 'Portugal', obviously, and something to the tune of 'Go West', and that seemed about it. Bless them.

It was still 1–0 at half-time, when the stadium announcer declared that the interval entertainment would be the 'Rhythm and Dance of Brazil', and let rip with some deafeningly loud samba music. Instinctively I stared at the pitch. There indeed was a visual feast, though not exactly what I'd been expecting. There were eleven blokes in grey T-shirts and tracksuit bottoms, treading down the grass. I didn't quite get it. Fair enough, they were quite good at it, but I was struggling to fit their movements to the rhythm of the music. I was still mulling over this concept, of how they'd managed to kill two birds with one stone by engaging for the half-time show a team of choreographed divot replacers to a Latin American beat, when out of the corner of my eye I spotted three powerfully built, dusky women in scanty, glittery costumes gyrating their way along the running track beside the pitch. They must have been the 'Rhythm and Dance of Brazil'; the choreographed middle-aged divot replacers I'd been so avidly watching were in fact the, er, divot replacers.

France's equaliser through Thierry Henry was greeted by enormous noise and the flashing appearance on the scoreboard of the word 'GOOL!', with pictures of footballs for the Os. Then the final whistle went and the entire corporate section I was sitting in stood up to leave. I pointed out to my neighbour that there would be extra time, he passed the word around and they all sat down again.

Everyone who followed the Euro 2000 tournament will be familiar with the dramatic end to the game, by Zidane's golden goal penalty three minutes before the end of extra time. I can't help feeling that the Portuguese, in the middle of all their disappointment the next morning, might feel just a little bit embarrassed about their protests to the referee when they came to watch the video. Xavier's handball was a cracking save, even if it was dubious as to whether the ball was going in.

I drove back to Holland straight after the game, to Deventer where I'd been working with Eurosupport, helping them get some media coverage for the work of the international fans' embassies. Next morning I decamped to Volendam, a tourist resort just outside Amsterdam, where I was to spend the last few nights of the tournament. Volendam is like a posh Dutch Whitby, a little fishing harbour that these days makes more of its money by selling itself as a taste of Old Holland. It's all hotels, restaurants and souvenir shops where you're expected to get yourself photographed in traditional Dutch costume and clogs. Like I was going to do that.

Having sorted out a hotel room, I headed back into Amsterdam, via the ArenA where I tried unsuccessfully to blag myself another credential for the second semi-final that evening. Apparently, and not entirely surprisingly, there were unlikely to be any empty seats for the Italy–Holland game, and the decision had been taken to supply fan coaches stadium accreditation only to fan co-ordinators of the countries involved in the game. Fair enough really, though I did try to convince them by referring to the 1,100 English fans who had tickets for the match and dropping dark hints about the mischief that any number of Englishmen could get up to without me to keep an eye on them.

Instead I ended up watching the dramatic exit of the host nation from the tournament in a small bar on the Nieuwendijk in the middle of Amsterdam. The pub was about the size of an average living room, and the clientele for this game eventually numbered about fifty, spilling onto the pavement outside. I got there fairly early and bagged a seat at the bar, as it turned out next to a Kiwi called Andrew who told me he was a beer importer and exporter. I waited for the punchline, but it never came, so presumably he was an importer and exporter of beer.

It was a typically Dutch experience. The locals present were mostly in their forties, I'd guess, and I'd also guess that when I got there they weren't on their first pint, if you get my drift. The bar was run by a couple with an airhorn (obviously vital in a room that size) and a dog with an orange scarf on. The outside of the bar was very orange, and inside everything that could be was decorated in, er, orange.

They cheered noisily at almost everything, and when there was a break in the play, they would play a blast on the CD of Dutch oompah music, very loudly. I tried to enter into the spirit of it all and smile broadly when the music played, at least for the first 30 or so times. It wasn't easy to keep up though, especially as every time the landlady caught my eye while I was smiling she would let off a blast on her airhorn, which in turn would set off the dog barking.

They cheered loudest of all when poor Zambrotta was sent off for a second bookable offence, a bit harsh as the replay had shown that in the incident for which he received the first booking, he had definitely played the ball.

Half-time entertainment was a bit different here. It consisted of 15 minutes of very loud oompah music, as an accompaniment to a tremendous balancing act, as the landlord stood on two stools, one on top of the other, to reach up and shorten the flex on the central light fitting, so that people right at the back could see the top of the screen. All around his precarious DIY turn, very drunk middle-aged Dutch people were singing, dancing, letting off airhorns and generally being very orange.

This was of course the game that the Dutch amazingly contrived to lose, all because of their abject failure with penalties. Two were missed during the ninety minutes, playing against ten men – Frank De Boer's saved, Kluivert's hitting a post. If they missed chances like that, they didn't deserve to go through to the final, I thought very quietly to myself – although given the din in the bar, I could have thought it quite loudly and no-one would have noticed.

Credit where it's due though, I thought the Italians defended superbly with their ten men. They seemed to be hanging on for penalties, but fair play to them, they did it extremely well and did what they set out to do. I made Cannavaro my unofficial man of the match, and made a mental note that next time I bumped into Bobby Robson I'd suggest that he signed him. Of course Bobby relies very heavily on me to supplement his sketchy knowledge of continental players . . .

The penalty shoot-out was only ever going to go one way, and its effect was dramatic, in that as it ended the bar fell silent and emptied very quickly. I took enormous pleasure in Jaap Stam's penalty miss in particular, and I was still smirking to myself when I walked out of the bar and almost literally bumped into Alan Curbishley and Garry Nelson. They asked me where Dam Square was from there; naturally, I didn't know.

I had the pleasure of the company of my wife Sandra and her friends (oops, that should of course read "our" friends) for the weekend of the final, and we filled the time before the Sunday playing at tourists. I was astonished at the change that came over Holland in those two days.

Right up until the semi-final, Holland had been football daft in general, and orange-mad in particular. There had been notices in most of the shop windows in Amsterdam announcing that the shop would be closing early on Thursday for the Euro 2000 semi-final; everything was bedecked in orange. By Friday morning, it had nearly all disappeared. Orange mania was turned off like a tap.

Maybe I noticed it more because my mind was attuned to it, but the contrast was remarkable. The scale of the orange obsession had been very pronounced before. There was orange everything available. All the things you'd expect, like hats. And shirts. And shorts. And flags. And socks. And mugs. And inflatable armchairs. And sunglasses. And bunting. And bedspreads. And pens. And key rings. And you get the picture.

But there were also a few other things I hadn't come across

before. Like inflatable orange clogs. And inflatable orange crowns – these produced by the Dutch FA. And inflatable orange windmill hats. And inflatable orange dinghies – except these weren't designed for taking to the water in, they were for sitting in front of the telly in. And orange head squares, with the words to the Dutch national anthem printed on.

And we saw an orange dog – I'm pretty sure it was originally white and had been dyed. And on the main road down towards Eindhoven – or more accurately, beside the main road – a farmer had marked out his cow field as a football pitch and dressed his herd in orange bibs. Passed at speed, they looked like particularly portly roadsweepers.

There had been some really imaginative thinking done by the creative boys in the red (orange?) braces. The marketing men at Amstel hit gold when they produced those football-shaped hats, a version for each competing team, complete with the appropriate national anthem lyrics printed on a label inside. They knocked the crappy things *The Sun* gives away into a plastic bowler.

Our favourite souvenir from Euro 2000 (though I'd hesitate to take a used one home) was the plastic goalposts positioned on an (orange) mat found in the urinals at the best bars. Attached to the crossbar is a little target, and the whole game is irresistible. It brought a whole new dimension to, er, urinating. Everyone had their own preferred techniques. Some people went for a "Uwe", which meant they sprayed it over the bar. A "Wanchope" meant you misjudged it and ended up trying to dribble it in. Really flash bastards would try a "Beckham"; they stand outside the toilet door and try to curl it round the wall. Me, I used to wait as long as I could until I was desperate to go, then really blast it, Shearer-style.

But as soon as the semi-final defeat, the whole lot disappeared. It was as if the entire nation was trying to deal with their disappointment by pretending they'd never been that bothered anyway. A bit like how you cope with being dumped when you're fourteen.

One shop on the Damrak in Amsterdam was dedicated to Dutch merchandise, all in orange, to the extent that most tourists thought it was called the 'Hup Holland' shop. I walked past it almost without noticing it on the Friday morning, the day after the semi. Out front, it had a brand new display of French merchandise.

So the anticipated big Dutch party in Amsterdam didn't materialise. All the concerns expressed by barge owners fearing the sinking of their boats by success-crazed, orange-painted Dutch football fans jumping on them to watch the victory parade were unnecessary. If it's possible for a major championship final to take place in an air of anti-climax, this one did. At least for the hosts; the French and Italians in town were quite excited. I admired one Frenchman's T-shirt. Bearing side by side pictures of the World Cup and the Euro 2000 trophy, it read '1998 – *Celle-la, on l'a deja.* 2000 – *Celle-ci, on l'aura*'. Quietly confident; I don't think the same thing would have worked in English.

Not that the game itself was in any way a let down. It was a great game, a fitting end to a great tournament. We watched it in a bar on the Rembrandtplein in Amsterdam. I went into the match almost neutral, if anything with a leaning towards the Italians as I didn't think they'd got the credit they deserved for beating the Dutch. But it was impossible not to admire the flair of the French team, and by half-time I was rooting decisively for them

It wasn't really the Frenchmen's flair that swayed me, though. It was the company in the bar.

There was a group of American students there, clearly in the middle of 'doing Europe' that summer. Strangely, they were really loud, arrogant, ignorant, self-important and annoying. I didn't take to them. And they were all supporting Italy. Noisily. Within half-an-hour of kick-off I'd come out for France. By half-time I was shouting for them. By the end of ninety minutes, I was ready to go to war for France. But only if the war was against these students.

I think the moment that clinched it for me was when, with Italy 1–0 up (my coming out for France was just the fillip they needed), the on-screen clock read 79 minutes gone, and one of the Americans shouted 'We've just about done it! There's only one minute to go!' Not one of his mates picked him up on it.

I was driving, so I wasn't drinking beer. I did get through eight Red Bulls though. It looked as though my early tip for player of the tournament, Del Piero, could have done with a can or two as well, as he missed two sitters. I'm grateful to him; he made that fantastic finale possible. Even though he did completely restore my confidence in my own inability to predict the game.

At the end of the game, the inflatable Frenchman at the end of the pitch was standing proud, huge and erect. Even though he had no face to speak of, he looked very pleased with himself.

Dutch television reported that 25 Italian neo-fascists had been arrested in Rotterdam. 16 policemen were injured in rioting in Paris at 1.00 am.

I got the ferry home from Europort to Hull on the Monday evening. In the bar prior to the journey I watched with admiration as two particularly ugly English blokes managed to sell France v Portugal semi-final commemorative T-shirts to a group of leather-clad gay German bikers. You couldn't make it up.

Looking Back, Thinking Forward

SO WHAT COULD be learnt from Euro 2000?

One obvious answer would be: how to play football. Forgetting for a moment England's performances, there had been some spectacular matches, some great football. OK, so the two non-England group games I went to also happened to be the only goalless games of the whole event – that was just my usual bad luck. Even I had managed to get in to see some memorable games, and I'd enjoyed some marvellous games on television.

The tournament had made some reputations, enhanced others. Luis Figo's eventual inflated transfer fee of 40 million pounds was due at least in part to his fantastic performances broadcast to an audience of hundreds of millions. There were some great individuals and teams on display. Portugal impressed a lot of people. Slovenia surprised a few. And there were the other oustanding individuals – Zidane, Henry and Blanc of France, Toldo and Nesta of Italy, Chivu of Romania, Davids and Kluivert of Holland, Philip Neville of England. (Well, he did stand out. But more of Phil Neville later.) And for most fans, the most important aspect of a tournament is whether or not the football is enjoyable. It was.

Commercially too, UEFA were proclaiming the tournament a massive success. Just before the semi-finals, they'd announced in Belgium that they had sold 94% of tickets up to that point, and had achieved a 90% occupancy rate. That percentage can clearly only have risen when the last three games are taken into account. Of course, there's another way of looking at those figures. 90% occupancy means that one in ten seats were left empty. For a match at the Roi Baudouin stadium in Brussels for example, say the Italy v Romania game, that's 5,000 empty seats – which just about tallies with my estimate of the unused capacity. Yet I was aware of three people at least who were left outside the ground despite being desperate to see the game – I know they were keen because they whinged about it for days afterwards.

So a second obvious lesson is that something needs to be done about the ticketing system. It's ridiculous that a tournament as good as this one, and as popular, should see most of its matches take place in grounds less than full to capacity. Let's have far more of the tickets sold straight to the most committed supporters at prices they can afford. Let's have a system designed to make life easy for the fans, not the bureaucrats or their accountants and bankers.

What about away from the stadia? There are two big issues here: entertainment and policing. They should be very separate issues; the former involving how to give the best possible all-round experience to the big majority of visitors, the latter how to cope with the minority who create problems. Unfortunately at Euro 2000 they once again became one issue, or more accurately the former went out of the window as all energies were poured into the latter.

There are a lot worse places to go for a football holiday than Holland in general, Amsterdam in particular. That's not really surprising, given that there is a massive influx of tourists into the Dutch capital anyway every weekend, even without a football match to go to. There are probably worse places to go than Brussels and Charleroi for a match too, though they don't spring to mind as readily. I don't think the Belgian Tourist

Board is particularly advantageously placed to be launching a new drive targetting English football fans right now, either from the point of view of cashing in on its reputation with potential visitors or in terms of the prospects of finding welcoming hosts.

But hosting a tournament is not the usual tourist run-of-the-mill. It is a very lucrative business, a special occasion for football fans, and it is not unreasonable to expect some special provision to be made to welcome and cater for football supporters. In my experience, those people directly involved in providing services to visiting supporters were extremely dedicated and hard-working. They were well-intentioned throughout, and achieved some notable successes. They were drawn from a variety of agencies – local authorities, interior ministries, fan projects – and often thrown together on an ad hoc basis, often working small miracles. But it was hard to avoid the impression that many of the services they were delivering were provided as an afterthought or a necessary but unfortunate overhead.

There were significant and marked differences in approach between the two host countries, which I think most England fans may just have noticed as manifested in the policing. But even in Holland, there was a tendency to regard fans as one of the problems that comes with hosting a tournament, rather than one of the reasons why tournaments exist in the first place. Clearly there is a case to be made for treating a section of fans, the hooligans, as a potential security problem, but if that approach extends to everybody, then not only does the tournament become less enjoyable than it could be for supporters, an opportunity is also missed to marginalise the problem element.

In words, the host countries and tournament organisers often made all the right noises, and used very positive phrases.

Football without Frontiers, for example. Apart from conjuring up extraneous memories of Eddie Waring introducing the mini-marathon, it seemed to set the right sort of tone. Ironic then, that the first border checks between Holland and Belgium for years were proposed during precisely this tournament. Frontiers because of Football, in practice.

There are different ways of telling that the authorities saw fans primarily as potential security problems. A quick glance at the official guide booklet for visiting supporters, 'Fans Only', gives an idea. (By the way, where on earth did they get that 'Fans Only' phrase from? What was it supposed to mean? It certainly didn't mean 'Just for genuine fans – no corporate sponsors'.) Open the guidebook and you see a page of contents, and a foreword. There's some basic information about fixtures and ticket allocation, and a guide to what the different bits of information on a ticket itself mean.

There then follows no fewer than NINE pages on security, detailing what the relevant laws are, what punishments can be expected, what's banned from stadia. In comparison, each host stadium gets only two pages, each host town another two.

For an even clearer picture, look at the finance figures. In the course of Euro 2000, over £100 million was spent on security. Less than £650,000 was spent on providing social and cultural events and services.

Again, Holland was much better than Belgium in terms of this sort of provision. In the Fans Only guide book, each Dutch city has a column detailing events organised for visitors during the tournament. There is in contrast not one single event listed in any of the Belgian cities. I know from visiting Charleroi before the tournament that other events were planned there; I know because I was told they had all been cancelled. It's all very well criticising the English for drinking all day, and I'm well aware that's quite possibly all many of us would have wanted to do anyway. The fact remains however that in Charleroi, that's all there was to do.

I do wonder though, in the case of some of the events and initiatives that were organised in the Dutch cities, who exactly they consulted about what football fans might like to see. In Arnhem, there was regular live music on a stage beside the big screen, which went down well; the same town however boasted in the guidebook of its 'parade of cows': 'at prominent places in the city, life-sized model cows, painted by local artists, will be displayed.' Amsterdam has lots of 'entertainment' of its own always, and added to the usual with street musicians in various squares throughout the city; they also held a 'barrel organ competition'. Still, variety is the spice of life, and they certainly made an effort.

The bottom line though is that there was a failure, in Belgium in particular, to make any distinction between the average supporter and the hooligan, and when both are to be treated the same, then it's understandable to err on the side of caution. But it's a short-sighted approach; instead of making it easier to isolate troublemakers, the end result is that it's the ordinary fan who becomes alienated.

Towards the end of the tournament – in other words when it was too late to make any difference – the Belgian authorities did admit that their approach had been indiscriminate, and offered half-hearted apologies to the innocent fans who'd suffered as a consequence. By then it was too late, the damage had been done. And I think it's certainly clear that innocent fans suffered. Apart from the ones whose testimony I've been able to include, there was the case too of the American rounded up and deported – to Manchester. And the Geneva businessman who'd won a 5-star trip to Euro 2000 in a magazine competition, and was deported on his first day there – to Manchester.

Of course it was not only the Belgian police who were unable – or unwilling – to differentiate between fans and hooligans. The Scottish *Sunday Mail* on 25th June reported the FSA's initiative to gather evidence from innocent fans who were the victims of injustice in Belgium like this:

> English thugs involved in riots at Euro 2000 have launched a brass-necked bid to clear their name. The Football Supporters' Association announced a campaign to protect 'innocent' football fans arrested by Belgian police from being branded as hooligans.

Not even the Belgian police claimed that the FSA were 'English thugs involved in riots at Euro 2000'. And while they admit that many of those they arrested, even battered, had done nothing wrong, Martin Kelner in *The Guardian* says he thinks it was 'a shame the Belgian riot police were not equipped with real bullets'.

So there are lessons about hosting tournaments. Think about the whole experience of supporters – it's not good enough for the football authorities to say 'we'll look after inside the stadia, anything outside is someone else's problem'. And stop regarding every arriving fan as a potential security headache.

None of which is to belittle the challenge that the Euro 2000 experience has set English fans. Clearly, there is an urgent need to rid football of racist violence. In fact I'd be so bold as to say I'd like to rid the whole of society of racist violence. Not just racist violence, but racism and violence. That's one of the reasons I get absolutely sickened by the sight and sound of all these politicians demanding draconian powers against football fans, when for the other eleven months of the year, they're stoking up racism in society generally with their outrageous attitudes towards the treatment of asylum seekers.

Let's not get hung up either on the idea that hooliganism is an exclusively English problem. True, the numbers of Britons arrested at Euro 2000 far exceeded those of any other country. But the English were the only fans targeted with a mayoral instruction (in Brussels) of 'arrest as many as you can'. Every other nation has its problems with hooliganism and racism too.

Consider for example these quotes from a report in the *Daily Express* of June 21st.

'Rampaging gangs set fire to police cars and buildings in a night of violence and madness.'

'Fans tried to storm it before being beaten back by riot police on foot and horseback firing rubber bullets. Hundreds of off-duty officers finally had to be called in to quell the violence in the city's banking and commercial heart.'

'A team spokesman said: "We are devastated that victory has been soured by some mindless behaviour, but the parade will go ahead."'

No, not more dire reports of 'England's Shame'. (I suppose the bit about the victory parade would have given that away.) This was a report about rioting in Los Angeles after the LA Lakers had WON basketball's NBA championship by beating Indiana Pacers. So let's not beat ourselves up too much with the idea that only England has any of these problems.

I'd say that the first step in trying to get rid of the racist thugs is to isolate them from the rest, by getting the majority on board. All the measures we've seen at Euro 2000 that treat everybody the same make that process much more difficult. So an end to indiscriminate measures that punish innocent and guilty alike would be a good starting point. Any successful policing anywhere depends on the support of the community to be policed. If they don't trust the police force, the policing can't work.

Before we go any further though, we need to be clear whether we believe there is a majority of football fans who can be mobilised against the racists and the thugs. I firmly believe there is, and I've seen plenty of evidence of positive fans' campaigns to be convinced it can be done. But I don't think that feeling is universally shared.

A lot of commentators have, perhaps subconsciously but often explicitly, written off all football fans as a hopeless case. To put it bluntly, I think there has been a lot of snobbery at work, sheer class prejudice at the thought of all those working-class blokes travelling abroad. Just look at all the sneering press references to beer bellies and tattoos, crew cuts and beer, written by precious upper middle-class journalists looking down from the balcony of their four-star hotel onto the rabble below. Or more likely, in the bar of their hotel miles away from the rabble in the cocooned atmosphere of the entourage of the team itself.

Confidence in the ordinary supporter lies at the base of my strategy for tackling these problems. There is no direct connection in my experience between being overweight with short hair, and being a racist hooligan. I met far more people with tattoos and drinking a lot who were appalled at the trouble caused by the few than who condoned it.

I reckon most supporters don't like the racist chanting and the violence. Their dislike usually remains passive though, and often with good reason. What is the decent fan supposed to do? They don't join in the racist chanting, but their silence still does not prevent the others being heard. It takes a brave individual to speak up in those circumstances. And when trouble starts among those committed to violence, what can an individual do to stop it, without adding to the violence or worse, becoming another victim of it?

Sooner or later, somebody does have to speak up and say 'we're not having this'. But if the individuals who do are to achieve more than martyrdom, then we need some organisation first. Those taking a stand – and I know there growing numbers prepared to do so – should be able to rely on the support of the great majority behind them. At the moment there is, I believe a latent sympathy, but it needs to be more than that. The sympathy needs to be built upon, consciously organised and given expression. This is of course a bit 'chicken and egg', in that sometimes to start motivating and organising the majority, there needs to be a few taking an initiative, but I think there will be plenty of volunteers in that direction. The FSA's Fans' Embassy is a case in point.

The best initiatives will come from below, from ordinary supporters, but there needs to be real encouragement from the top, from the football authorities. The first step would be to involve supporters and supporters' organisations in real dialogue. There have been some steps forward in this department in recent years – the involvement of the England Members Club in some of the FA's campaigns is a good example, and the FA and others have also been involved in their Euro 2000 working group. But it needs to go a lot further. A crucial element of the FSA's Embassy's success is that it is entirely independent of the football authorities, that it's run by fans, for fans. The FA needs to develop a much more mature relationship with supporters' groups, and it could start by accepting that it cannot always pick the representatives it wants.

A crucial next step would be the development of unified and fully funded supporters' organisations. For years the football authorities have used as an excuse for not consulting with or funding independent supporters' organisations the fact that the existing structures were too divided and diverse. Over the last couple of years, a lot of progress has been made in drawing fans' groups together. The Coalition of Football Supporters has united in action the FSA, the National Federation of Football Supporters' Clubs, several Independent Supporters' Associations and dozens of fanzines, and further progress seems likely, as evidenced by the joint work on the Euro 2000 embassy. But all the movement has been on the side of the fans; it has yet to be met with positive backing from those in charge of the game.

Adequate funding of fans' organisations would enable all sorts of initiatives to be developed to encourage a more positive culture among English fans. More fans travel abroad with club sides each year than with the national team, and many have already developed a positive image; there's no reason I can see why the same process could not take place around Team England.

There needs to be some investment in developing a new ethos around following England. Maybe the first step should be for a fans' organisation to start talking to the genuine supporters and find out what they want out of their England experiences. It would involve a lot of time and probably some money, but surely it's so important to the future of the game that even those making the money could see the value of spending some of it in this way.

We also need a sense of proportion about what can be achieved. I don't think the whole burden of determining what Englishness is can be put at the door of the FA and the England football team. The bigger problems of racism and violence among sections of the population are issues for the whole of society. There has always been a problem involving a section of men and fighting. Of course the football authorities need to be involved in dealing with these issues as they impact on football. But maybe the best way to proceed is to remember that Team England is exactly that – it's a football team. They don't have to take on all the baggage of deciding a national identity. Most fans travelling with Team England just want to support a football team – preferably a successful one, but if necessary we'll settle for one with Phil Neville in it.

Just stop to think about it – would any other football club come up with Jerusalem, or anything like it, as a team song? I very much doubt it. It reflects this attitude that they have to represent the whole nation, not just a football team. But in a situation where all sorts of commentators – social and political, not just football – are talking about the crisis of 'Englishness' against the background of devolution and European integration, is it realistic to expect a sporting body that has enough trouble getting its players to behave to take on the job of forging a new national identity?

(There are perhaps signs that, inadvertently maybe, the FA has begun to take the first tentative steps towards putting the footballing interests of 'Team England' before some abstract notion of national pride or misplaced patriotism. Kevin Keegan's resignation after the Wembley World Cup qualifier against the Germans – I'm sure I'm not the only one that felt the Germans' victory had an air of inevitability about it; normal service has been resumed – has left a vacancy to be filled as team coach, and the FA are having to come to terms with the idea that perhaps the best person for the job might not be English.

To me there's no big dilemma here; the FA should

appoint the best possible candidate to bring about a long-lasting improvement in the quality and achievements of Team England. This is one post where there are no international rules about who's eligible, no need to rummage through history books to check granny's place of birth, so why impose unnecessary constraints on ourselves?

Of course there all sorts of objections being raised about the idea of a non-English coach, not least the oft-repeated one that 'it's a telling comment on the sad state of English football if we need to look to a foreigner to run the national team'. I can't help thinking that there have been plenty of telling comments on the sad state of English football recently without worrying unduly about one more – if Euro 2000's nightmares have been expunged from the memory already, then the 0-0 in Helsinki was a ready reminder. And surely the priority is not to avoid telling comments, but to improve the sad state.

If appointing a non-English manager would be a disaster, then all I can say is that Team England could do with a similar sort of disaster to the ones that have befallen Manchester United, Arsenal, Leeds and Liverpool since they got their non-English bosses. And when I look at some of the characters who I've heard say that a foreign coach would mean the end of their following England abroad, well that's another positive reason for advertising the post in *L'Equipe* or the *Gazetta della Sport*.)

It is possible for football to have some impact on social problems. Many clubs – and the FA, to be fair – have come up with very effective campaigns on racism, say, which have made real progress on that issue, (though there's still a long way to go, and to paraphrase the finance company adverts, racism can go up as well as down).

There are lessons to be learnt from the anti-racism campaigns. The best ones start from the bottom up, and are run by fans. They are far more effective than anything that seems to be preaching from above. Also while there has been legislation introduced giving powers to deal with racists, the legal side has not been the central or even the most successful weapon. The crucial part has been convincing people there is another way to do things, winning their hearts and minds and creating the right sort of climate. In fighting racism, part of that has been done by the success of black players, showing how positive multi-racial teams and societies can be. Maybe for England fans, there has to be more investment in the positive, demonstrating in practice what a positive experience supporting Team England can be. That may mean spending money, but there's plenty of that knocking about in football. Let's have some investment in making travelling with Team England a pleasant experience, helping fans to interact positively with the locals and fans of other countries. Ask fans what they want, develop some positive role models, involve the players, treat fans with respect, presume they want to join in positively until they demonstrate otherwise, rather than the other way round. I genuinely believe that most England fans would be keen to re-assert a much more benign image of themselves, given support and encouragement.

It would also mean the FA sticking up for genuine supporters much more readily, rather than rushing to be the first and most vehement to condemn. I thought it was a disgrace that while EMC members were being arrested and deported without having put a foot wrong, all the FA spokespersons could do from their five-star hotel rooms was to endorse the police actions. Presumably in order to try to salvage its doomed World Cup 2006 bid. We want to try to divide the thugs from the rest, not contribute to the lumping together.

And the same goes for the government in dealing with the bigger picture. After Euro 2000, the government rushed into bad knee-jerk legislation, which renders football supporters the first group of people in Britain no longer presumed innocent until convicted by a court of law with an opportunity to defend themselves. They said publicly they'd be consulting with fans' organisations; in practice, it never happened. Now the same sort of bad law exists in Britain that the innocent English fans fell foul of in Belgium; there are hundreds of fans who've had their Euro 2000 destroyed, and now face the prospect of being banned from travelling again. It must not be allowed to happen. The government should immediately declare that it will not ban anyone from travelling to future matches just because they were deported from Belgium. If fans are guilty of offences, fine, then prosecute them in court, where they can defend themselves. And if they're convicted, ban them from coming to games. If we don't do it this way, we have hundreds of examples from this tournament of why it would be dangerous to go further.

No-one suffers more from football hooliganism and violence than genuine supporters. It's our game that's poisoned by the racism. We are the ones likely to get caught up in a fight we don't want, or get arrested, presumed guilty by proximity if not association. Most football fans are natural allies in the fight to rid football of violence, not part of the problem. We can be trusted to do our bit to look after the game we love.

There was one other thing – what was it? Ah yes, Philip Neville. Oh, it doesn't matter. Bless him, he's probably suffered enough for that tackle. I know I have.

Appendix

The Lowdown Quiz (page 25)

1 Tony Woodcock, Ian Storey-Moore, Peter Osgood.

2 Mike Duxbury, Graham Rix, Kerry Dixon, Lee Dixon, Jason Willcox, Graeme le Saux.

3 Alan Shearer, Paul Scholes, Michael Owen, Steve McManaman, Gareth Southgate.

4 Paul Stewart

5 The Brazilian congress declared him a 'national treasure', thus forbidding his sale overseas.

6 Hit the woodwork.

7 Crystal Palace

8 Weight. Having clearly eaten all the pies, he was the fattest of the lot at 15st 10lbs.

9 Grimsby – they play in Cleethorpes.

10 Leeds Utd.

11 Gary McAllister

12 Coventry in 1987

The Lowdown Quiz No. 2 (page 82)

1 Portsmouth, 1939–1946

2 Swindon Town

3 Anderlecht

4 George Best, in 1970 at Boothferry Park

5 FC Liege

6 Eyal Berkovic

7 One of the QPR players had meningitis

8 He scored the fastest ever international goal, after 8.3 seconds against England in 1993

9 John Barnes, with Watford, Liverpool and Newcastle

10 Manchester United, Arsenal, Leeds, Liverpool, Chelsea, Leicester, Bradford and Aston Villa.

The Even Lower Down Quiz (page 175)

1 Arsenal, Scunthorpe Utd and Manchester F**king Utd.

2 Halifax, Exeter, Oxford Utd, Wrexham and Crewe Alexandra.

3 John Lukic's mum (she was an air hostess on the Munich plane)

4 Enzo Scifo

5 Stan Collymore, Carlton Palmer, Paul Ince, Neil Ruddock, Mark Hughes and Dean Saunders

6 Colour in the letters in the home side's name

7 They're brothers-in-law

8 Dan Petrescu

9 Imre Varadi

10 Ian Botham and Denis Law

Belgian Police Wordsearch (page 183)

Indiscriminate, administrative, arrests, water cannon, teargas, terrible, over the top, cordon, horses, muzzles, bad, beer, attack, absent, riot, helmet, truncheon, rash, Poirot, shield, overreaction, complacency, power crazed, heavy-handed, spraying, id checks.

EURO 2000: The Results

GROUP A

Germany 1 – 1 Romania	(June 12th, Liege)
Portugal 3 – 2 England	(June 12th, Eindhoven)
Romania 0 – 1 Portugal	(June 17th, Arnhem)
England 1 – 0 Germany	(June 17th, Charleroi)
England 2 – 3 Romania	(June 20th, Charleroi)
Portugal 3 – 0 Germany	(June 20th, Rotterdam)

GROUP B

Belgium 2 – 1 Sweden	(June 10th, Brussels)
Turkey 1 – 2 Italy	(June 11th, Arnhem)
Italy 2– 0 Belgium	(June 14th, Brussels)

Sweden 0 – 0 Turkey	(June 15th, Eindhoven)
Turkey 2 – 0 Belgium	(June 19th, Brussels)
Italy 2 – 1 Sweden	(June 19th, Eindhoven)

GROUP C

Spain 0 – 1 Norway	(June 12th, Rotterdam)
Yugoslavia 3 – 3 Slovenia	(June 13th, Charleroi)
Slovenia 1 – 2 Spain	(June 18th, Amsterdam)
Norway 0 – 1 Yugoslavia	(June 18th, Liege)
Slovenia 0 – 0 Norway	(June 21st, Arnhem)
Yugoslavia 3 – 4 Spain	(June 21st, Bruges)

GROUP D

France 3 – 0 Denmark	(June 11th, Bruges)
Netherlands 1 – 0 Czech Rep.	(June 11th, Amsterdam)
Czech Rep. 1 – 2 France	(June 16th, Bruges)
Denmark 0 – 3 Netherlands	(June 16th, Rotterdam)
Denmark 0 – 2 Czech Rep.	(June 21st, Liege)
France 2 – 3 Netherlands	(June 21st, Amsterdam)

QUARTER FINALS

Italy 2 – 0 Romania	(June 24th, Brussels)
Turkey 0 – 2 Portugal	(June 24th, Amsterdam)
Spain 1 – 2 France	(June 25th, Bruges)
Netherlands 6 – 1 Yugoslavia	(June 25th, Rotterdam)

SEMI FINALS

| France 2 – 1 Portugal | (June 28th, Brussels) |
| Italy 0 – 0 Netherlands | (June 29th, Amsterdam) |

Italy win 3–1 on penalties

FINAL

| France 2 – 1 Italy | (July 2nd, Rotterdam) |